LI

GW01418698

UNDER FIVE FLAGS.

MY LIFE & MINISTRY IN

CHALLENGING TIMES.

BOOK THREE.

CALLED TO BE AN OVERCOMER!

ZIMBABWE TO ENGLAND.
By

Alan (AB) Robertson

Living Under Five Flags-Book Three

© 2021 by Alan (AB) Robertson

ISBN 978-1-8384255-7-9
Published by Caracal Books
United Kingdom. https://www.facebook.com/CaracalBooks

The internet addresses, email addresses, and phone numbers in this book are accurate at the time of publication.

Photos-Maps-© Colin Weyer
www.rhodesia.me.uk

Flag and Map

FOREWORD

Whilst reading this book I marvel firstly at the absolute sovereignty of God who says, "I am the Lord that maketh all things" (Isaiah 44:24), and, "yet will I not forget thee" (Isaiah 49:15), and the words of the Apostle Paul in Galatians 1:15 "But when it pleased God, who separated me from my mother's womb, and called me by His grace, TO REVEAL HIS SON IN ME, that I might preach Him ....". I also see the same amazing grace and divine sovereignty of the One and only living God over and over, in our own lives too, especially in the last fleeting forty or fifty years covered by AB's writings here. Hallelujah! What a wonderful and amazing God we serve. Amen.

Secondly, I recall the miracle of the man born blind in the Gospel of John chapter 9. A man born at that time and in that way, "that the works of God should be made manifest in him". A man born into those particular circumstances and that individual situation at that specific time so that the works of God should be made manifest in him through Christ Jesus. Now, looking back over the past forty to fifty years and reading this book written by AB Robertson, I see the sovereign works of God manifest in our lives and in our times in just the same way as those written about in the Gospel of John in AD69.

My transfer to CID Special Branch Chipinga in 1979 while AB Robertson was the minister of the Chipinga Assembly of God was no coincidence. From AB's short time in Chipinga, we witnessed that small assembly equip and send seven people into ministry, of which I was one. I returned from The Bible College of

Wales in late 1982 and in 1983 Rina and I joined AB and Mally to serve in ministry as assistants at Bethshan Assembly in Bulawayo. Today, forty years later, those seven are still serving our Lord. That speaks of lasting fruit that remains. Fruit that came to full ripeness and remains to this day.

The Assemblies of God as a movement continues to play a major role in ours and many other lives. We praise our Heavenly Father for His instruments. AB Robertson is indeed a spiritual father to us and many others.

Soon and very soon we are all going to see our King. What a day, what a glorious day that will be! Together in the service of Jesus Christ forever. Amen.

Simon Rhodes (Johannesburg RSA 2021)

AB Robertson,

FRIEND, COLLEAGUE AND LEADER OF MEN.

The task of leading the New Covenant Assemblies of God fell to AB during the troubled and turbulent times in the new and emerging country of Zimbabwe. He led us through the birth pangs of the political, economic and spiritual upheaval that we all encountered as the new nation emerged.

There was the ever changing, and unprecedented emigration situation as people left the country in huge droves. This placed real and constant pressure upon the Churches and those who remained. Income streams dried up as families and Ministers relocated to other parts of the world. There was the constant need to find experienced Godly men to fulfill the spiritual vacuum for those left behind, with constantly dwindling resources.

Through it all, AB led us with unflinching resolve. He became a father figure to young ministers like myself as his steady hand guided us through these tempestuous and tumultuous times! He instilled in us faith, hope and confidence in God and the future.

While in Kadoma in 1989, AB and others encouraged me to stand as a member of the National Executive of the NCAOG in Zimbabwe. As a result, I was privileged to serve on the National Executive along with Billy Nel, John Baker, and Stuart Macdonald. At the same time, I was also the pastor of the Redcliff Assembly and had seven local churches come under my leadership. It was a daunting task and I would never have had the confidence to do it without the superb support and encouragement of the entire Executive and AB's urging.

This book is a detailed account of the battles and victories we all encountered

A nostalgic look back at wonderful friends, challenging times and the glorious demonstrations of God's love and faithfulness.

Robbie Burns

(Pastor in New Zealand)

INTRODUCTION

As mentioned in the introduction to Books One and Two, I was asked by Tim King to write the "foreword" of his book **"IN SEARCH OF OPHIR."** This dealt with the history of the Assemblies of God in Rhodesia/Zimbabwe between 1952-1985. I did as I was requested, but also provided additional information about my own ministry throughout Zimbabwe. As Tim's book was already completed, he suggested I write my own book, and **'LIVING UNDER FIVE FLAGS'** has been the result.

In Book One, I dealt with my early years, living under the Southern Rhodesian flag. This was followed by explaining how the Lord called me into the ministry during the days when the Rhodesian flag flew confidently over our country. In Book Two I dealt with my life as a Minister of the Gospel from 1972-1980 in the country now called Zimbabwe. During those years I lived under a number of different flags, the Rhodesian, Zimbabwe-Rhodesia, the Union Jack (for a short season) and finally the flag of Zimbabwe.

This final book records the time when I was the minister of Bethshan Tabernacle in Bulawayo and continues after I became the leader of the English Language work in the country. Initially I continued to be the senior minister at Bethshan but I then moved to McChlery Avenue Assembly in Harare. My story concludes with our final year in Bulawayo before moving to the United Kingdom.

As it happens, this has been the most difficult part of my story to relate. However, from an historical point of view it is possibly the most important. It was an amazing period starting at the beginning of 1983 and ending in December 1989. It was a time of great change but I suppose none of us realised just how much everything was changing. We made mistakes and as we look back at those years it is possible that we could have done things a little differently. However, history is history, we cannot change it even if we wish that we could.

In conclusion I want to thank the Lord for all those wonderful men and women that I had the privilege of working with during those eventful years. Some of them have been mentioned during the course of relating my story and my apologies to those who have not been mentioned. We may not have always seen eye to eye, nevertheless it was a great honour to have served the Lord with all of them during that time. They have all enriched my life for which I am truly grateful.

My task in the service of King Jesus is still not fully completed,

THE UNFINISHED TASK.

Alan (AB) Robertson

Chapter 1

BETHSHAN TABERNACLE

BULAWAYO 1980-1982

Up to now in LIVING UNDER FIVE FLAGS, we have been using the 'old names' of the towns and cities of the land of my birth. However, as we move into this new phase of my story, I will be using the 'NEW NAMES.' These are the names that were chosen by the new administration and applied as soon as they were able to do so. However, you will notice that the name of the city of my birth did not change. BULAWAYO, was King Lobengula's Capital when the white man first arrived in the country and the name was never changed. It remains the second city of Zimbabwe and the largest city in Matabeleland.

Since entering the ministry in 1972, I had been privileged to serve the Lord my God all over Zimbabwe. My first posting was as an assistant minister in Shurugwe and Gweru, this was followed by my being assistant minister at McChlery Avenue in Harare. I then had the privilege of having my own church and ministering in Kwe Kwe, followed by Hatfield in Harare, Mutare, and finally Chipinge. But late in 1980, I was returned home to Bulawayo to become the minister of Bethshan Tabernacle.

After leaving Chipinge we did not go directly to Bulawayo but headed first of all for a much-needed holiday by the sea in South Africa. Our destination on this occasion was COPES COTTAGE on the south coast of Natal.

COPES COTTAGE BALLITOVILLE NATAL.

In was early in the 1970's that John Bond arranged to have a biannual conference for all the ministers and leaders who looked to him for leadership. These conferences were essential as the 'work' was expanding rapidly and congregations were scattered from Cape Town at the tip of South Africa to Harare and other centres in Zimbabwe. These 'conferences' were always a real blessing and were wonderful times of refreshing. There is much that I could say about these occasions, however I mention them here for one specific purpose.

On one of our visits to the CYARA CONFERENCE CENTRE in the Transvaal we learned about a 'holiday cottage' which was available for no charge or a very minimal charge. A Mr. Cope owned the 'cottage' and when he and his family were not using it, he made it available so that Ministers in the AOG could have an inexpensive sea side holiday with their wives and families.

As a result, having obtained his permission, when we left Chipinge in October 1980, we headed for 'COPES COTTAGE.' This was in Ballitoville which was not far from Durban on the South coast of Natal. I am not sure what we were expecting but this was no cottage! It was a large 'double story' house with a garage down below. It was not far from the beach and a great place to have a holiday. The Lord had truly blessed us and we were very thankful for the generosity of Mr. Cope!

While there we came across Luke du Plessis and his wife who were enjoying a caravan holiday a short distance away. They were long time Pentecostals who had been in fellowship with the Full Gospel Church in Kadoma before moving to Kwe Kwe and joining our Assembly. For many years they had looked after their son who was confined to a wheelchair. Sadly, he had suffered brain damage when, as an adult, he fell off a balcony and from then on needed constant care. Despite the obvious difficulties that they experienced caring for their adult son, they continued to praise and worship their Lord. They were a great example to us all and a real blessing, and it was wonderful to spend time with them in Ballitoville.

But it was not long before our holiday came to an end and we were once again on the road and travelling back home. Sadly, this was not to Rhodesia, or even Zimbabwe/Rhodesia we were now living under a different flag, we were going home to Zimbabwe. But, Despite the changed circumstances, Bulawayo was my home town, so it truly was 'going home' for me.

WELCOME HOME!

Before asking us to take on the Assembly in Bulawayo, Neil Gibbs, who was now leading the work under John Bond's leadership, had asked Steve Bacon to move to Bethshan. But Steve and Eve were not at all happy in Bulawayo, and within three months they moved back to Harare. It is only now, while writing my story, that I have suddenly realised, **"I was not the first choice for**

the job!"

However, despite not being the first choice for the job, it appeared that the Robertson's were going up in the world. Up until then, we had not been all that concerned about where we lived as long as we had a roof over our heads. Mally may have disagreed with that statement, however she never complained! As I have mentioned, Kwe Kwe had it's 'bucket toilet' in the garden outside, and the house in Mutare had its own special characteristics! It is true that both houses in Chipinge had been more than acceptable and the second house was really great, but, the house in Bulawayo at 90 Penrith Road, Morningside, was a really lovely house and we were very blessed to live there.

During the night of the 9th- 10th November 1980, we were woken by gun fire! It could well have been the very first night that we slept in our new house! Just in case you are wondering, it was not the hot water boiler, or avocado pears falling on the roof, in this case it was real! This was real gunfire, and a lot of it! Yet, once we were sure that it was not in close proximity to the house, we prayed about the situation, and then went back to sleep. We had often heard gunfire in the distance when we lived in Chipinge.

It was only later the next day that we discovered what had taken place. We learned that fighting had broken out between groups of fighters from the Zimbabwe African National Liberation Army, (ZANLA) and others from the Zimbabwe People's Revolutionary Army. (ZIPRA) A four-hour gunfight had taken place between men who were loyal to Joshua Nkomo, (ZIPRA) and men who were loyal to our new

Prime Minister Robert Mugabe (ZANLA). It only came to an end when the largely 'white- led' BSAP Support Unit intervened on behalf of the government. This became known as 'ENTUMBANE I' as the main clashes had taken place in Bulawayo's western suburb of Entumbane.

We were HOME, what a welcome to my home town!!

The following year 'ENTUMBANE II' took place between the 8th and the 12th of February. This was a much more serious uprising, and was once again, only put down by military personnel who had been part of the former Rhodesian Army. The Russians, who had backed Joshua Nkomo throughout the 'bush war,' had amongst other weapons, supplied him with a number of tanks. It appears that during this time he and his men tried to take over Bulawayo, however, he failed to take into account the former Rhodesian Army which were based in the city. The Russian tanks were only stopped because these well-trained military personnel were still in existence and prevented the tanks from entering the city. I have recently discovered that the Russian T-34 tanks were later found to be non-functional. However, no one knew that before the battle.

LEANDER & HILLSIDE INFANTS SCHOOLS.

Our eldest son, Mark, turned five years old the same month that we arrived in Bulawayo. That January, the beginning of the school year, he started school at Leander Infant School. It was difficult to purchase school clothes his size when he started school as he was really quite small but, we finally succeeded. He was one of the youngest in his class and truly loved his new school.

The school had been established as a 'Community School' with a high degree of parental involvement. The parents wanted to protect the students from what they considered to be the inevitable fall in standards, now that the new government had taken over. Although it was largely a 'white school' the idea was not to exclude 'black' students but rather to maintain acceptable standards. But, sadly, after only one term, the new government closed the school down. Although Mark loved his school, he was required to move to Hillside Infants, part of Hillside Junior School. Praise God, the school was not far from home and proved to be equally as good as Leander. For different reasons, this proved to be the first of many moves that Mark would be required to make before he finally left school.

Leander Infants School and Hillside Junior School
Taken around 1998 when Mally and I visited
Zimbabwe from the UK

BETHSHAN TABERNACLE

Despite the 'warm welcome' that we had been given coming home to Bulawayo, it was great being part of Bethshan Tabernacle which had a very healthy congregation. The Assembly had been established for some years and we were blessed to have a couple of good elders in the fellowship. One of elders was Graham Whiting who had been such a blessing to me during my early Christian walk in what is now Harare, and the other was Dennis Poole. Both men had attended the Assemblies of God Bible College at Kenly in England and were a great asset to the Assembly.

It was particularly good to work with Graham again and he and his family were a real blessing to the assembly. However, he did say to me after one Bible study that my teaching was more in keeping with a Bible College than a local church. He also let me know when I arrived, that he had served under 'many kings' during his time as an elder. He was of course referring to the different ministers who had laboured at McChlery and at Bethshan. One of those 'kings' was Paddy McCoun who remained at Bethshan for a short time before he moved on. Sadly, in hindsight I think we would have made a good team had he stayed.

While at Bethshan, Paddy started a NEW BELIEVER'S BIBLE STUDY which we continued to lead in the lounge of our new home. A number of these people became real stalwarts in the work of God as time went on, and as a result of these weekly meetings we all became very close. Some of those attending had just been 'saved' but others just wanted a 'refresher' course and of course all were welcome.

Like Chipinge, our time at Bethshan was very full and so I will deal with the major things that happened and some other incidents that come to mind. One of those incidents was when the telephone rang one day and the voice at the end of the line said, "**Good afternoon I wonder if you could assist us? We are driving home from Victoria Falls on our way to Harare, and are just outside Bulawayo and have run out of petrol. We have money, but the garage on the Fall's Road is completely out of fuel and as a result we are really stuck. Could you get us some petrol and bring it out to us and we will pay you whatever it costs? I am with my wife and family and we really need some assistance. We are believers and are in fellowship with ------ in Harare.**"

Although I did not know the man at the other end of the line I responded and set out on my rescue mission and praise God, they were soon on their way. I am not sure whether they spent a few days in Bulawayo at that time, or whether they returned sometime later, but, somewhere along the line we visited Matobo National Park together. He was a professional photographer and took some absolutely fantastic pictures of our family in the park. Among the photo's that he took was one at Rhodes Grave, and another at the Allan Wilson Memorial. He also took an amazing photo of Mark, Matthew and Jonathan, at our dinner table in Bulawayo. These photos are without doubt the best photos that were ever taken of our sons when they were young.

Having moved into a lovely house in Bulawayo we were also blessed to see a significant improvement in our furniture. We had only just settled in when someone from our congregation offered us a lovely lounge suite at a reasonable price which we decided to buy. The 'yellow' lounge suite, given to us as a gift, when we first moved to Umtali, had seen good service, but it was time for a change. In addition, we acquired a Welsh Dresser, dining room table and chairs, which were in lovely condition, when my mother and uncle Fred sold up and moved to Cape Town in South Africa. We were very grateful to the Lord for His abundant provision!

The Boys at our table in Bulawayo.

New to the congregation were Bernard Maddock and his wife Ann, who were regulars at Bethshan. Every now and again Bernard would come around to the house on his shiny Honda motor cycle. On one of his visits Bernard took a lovely photograph of Mark and Matthew sitting on his Honda with Mally (holding Jonathan), and myself standing behind his bike. It must have been as a result of his influence that I purchased a Suzuki 125cc soon after arriving in Bulawayo as a second set of wheels. I was able to take Mark to school every morning on the back of my bike.

I soon discovered that Geoff Gonifas who was ministering at Belleview Assembly was also travelling on two wheels, and possessed a Yamaha 125cc Motorcycle. I am not sure when, but it was while we were still living in Bulawayo, that I traded in my set of wheels for another new motorcycle, this time a Yamaha 125cc. Both bikes were a joy to me but they could never match the joy that I had received from my original Honda 150cc motorcycle when I first started work.

One day while at Bethshan, I preached on the importance of 'work,' and stressed what the Apostle Paul had written to the Thessalonian Church in his second letter,

"-----. If anyone will not work, neither shall he eat." 2 Thessalonians 3.10

At the end of the service, a young man came up to me with tears in his eyes, deeply moved by what I had said. He explained that he had done everything to get a job, he had personally walked all around the industrial and commercial areas of Bulawayo and no one was prepared to give him a job. We spent some time in conversation and then prayed together. Praise God, the Lord saw his tears and within a short time he was gainfully employed.

I was surprised to discover when reading Tim King's book, "IN SEARCH OF OPHIR," that what became the 6th Avenue Assembly had actually started in Waterford. But the 6th Avenue Assembly no longer existed as some years before my arrival in Bulawayo it had amalgamated with Bethshan.

Despite that, Bob and Sheila Wood and their family who were in fellowship with us at Bethshan still ran a Sunday School for the local children in Waterford.

From the first day of the establishment of the Sunday School, it had only catered for 'white' children as Waterford was a 'white' suburb. However, since 1979 things had been changing and 'black' residents were buying up properties and moving into the area. This created a bit of a problem with some of the parents, when 'black' children started attending the Sunday School. One day when I was discussing the situation with Bob Wood, I said something like the following' **"Bob, the situation in the country has changed. As a result, the situation in Waterford has changed and whether we like it or not, WE HAVE TO CHANGE!"**

I was really proud of this wonderful Christian man and his dear wife Sheila and their family because they did 'change!' In fact, things changed so much that within a very short time almost every child in the Sunday School was 'black' and the Woods continued to love and care for each one. In fact, years later in addition to running the Sunday School they were also running a feeding scheme for the poor people living in the surrounding area. The last time Mally and I visited Zimbabwe we were present when they were doing this very thing. Praise God for this wonderful family.

While we are with the Woods, I need to mention something else. Because of the International sanctions that had been placed upon Rhodesia after our government declared independence from Britain in 1965 it had become very difficult to purchase 'drinking glasses' in the country. Mr. Wood came up with a plan where he turned empty bottles of all kinds into drinking glasses. He cut off the top portion, smoothed off the glass and what was left was a fine drinking glass. They were much in demand from hotels, bars and restaurants as well as private individuals. The top portion of the bottle was also utilised, but I have forgotten how. It is amazing what we can do when we have no other choice.

THE ABSENTEE PREACHER AND A PACKED CHURCH.

I am not too sure when this took place, but one day I was asked if we could host a well-known American preacher at a special meeting at Bethshan. I had not met this brother before, however, I had heard his name mentioned on many occasions when moving around the country. He was well recommended and as a result I was only too happy to oblige.

It seemed that he was well-known in Bulawayo and news of his coming must have been widely circulated, as on the night of the meeting the church was packed. But, despite an extended time of worship provided by our excellent musicians he failed to turn up! As time went on, I came to the conclusion that we had to do something! We could not let all these people return home without hearing God's Word! As a result, I concluded that I would have to minister in his place, and so after a few minutes alone with the Lord I addressed the congregation. It was the largest congregation I had during the whole time I was at Bethshan and I praised God for the opportunity.

Our 'guest speaker' did finally arrive, but only after the meeting was over, and offered the following explanation, **"I do apologise for not being here for the meeting, but, I have quite a story to relate. We boarded the plane in Harare and were ready for takeoff, when we were told that there was a problem** and our flight would be delayed. After waiting on the plane for what seemed like ages, we were told to disembark as the aircraft would not be taking off at all. Sometime later we were told that another aircraft had been prepared for our flight and we were invited to board the new plane. Believe it or not there was another problem, this time with our replacement plane and our flight was once again delayed. Eventually that problem was resolved and we were able to leave. As you can imagine by this time all the passengers were very nervous, but praise God, we arrived safely, although a number of hours late. Once again my apologies."

By the way, we must have sent someone to the airport to meet him and were advised from time to time that his flight was delayed and so whilst we waited we were not completely in the dark. The details of this story may not be fully accurate but it was very similar to what I have related. As we move to the next story this may well have happened at a different time nevertheless, I am including it at this juncture.

THE LAWNMOWER AND THE FRIDGE.

It was Saturday morning and I needed to mow the lawn, but the lawn mower would not start. We had an old petrol mower at this stage and no matter what I did it would not start. I do not know about you, but I am not a very good handy man and when it failed to start, I became increasingly discouraged. I knew that I needed some help but it was late on a Saturday morning and I could not take it to a mechanic to get it fixed. In addition, as I considered all the people that I knew in Bulawayo, I really could not think of one person who I could phone and ask for help. The more I considered my situation the more I became discouraged. (It is amazing how such a little problem can cause such distress)

I do not remember if I prayed, but the Lord certainly saw my need. It was at that exact time that the Lord sent another minister to our home to encourage me. He happened to be visiting Bulawayo that weekend and told me that the Lord had laid Mally and I on his heart. He was a real blessing to both of us that morning, a 'messenger of the Lord!' He prayed with us, and encouraged us in that moment of discouragement. Despite that, sadly, I failed to ask him whether he knew anything about lawnmowers!!!

This was not the only time that the Lord sent someone specifically to meet our need. Sometimes we fail to recognise the people that the Lord places across our path to bless us. Praise God, He knows our every need, and will not forget us!

It was Christmas Eve, and we had just discovered that the fridge was not working and the chances of getting it fixed so late in the day and on Christmas Eve were pretty well zero. As it is very hot in Bulawayo at that time of the year, and the fridge and deep freeze contained more than the normal amount of food, I had made an effort to set up some sort of cooling system to help to preserve our food. It was at that point, having done my best, that visitors arrived at our front door.

We opened the door to Percy and Jean Hastings who were members of our congregation. They had come around to drop off a Christmas present for the family. Having thanked them for their gift, we invited them in and told them about our problem. Percy immediately climbed back into his car and returned sometime later with a fridge that he had taken out of their caravan. The fridge turned out to be a real blessing and saw us through the Christmas period. Once again, the Lord had met our need and once again, possibly, before we had really even prayed. God is so good!

THE DEATH OF MY STEPFATHER.

It was while we were in Bulawayo that we received news of the death of my stepfather. As mentioned earlier, he and my mother had sold up and moved to Cape Town. My stepfather had assisted his son with the purchase price of a lovely house that had a very nice 'granny flat' attached. He had effectively paid for the 'granny flat' where the two of them would be living. It gave them their own 'front door,' but they were near enough to his son Malcolm and his wife Maureen if they needed assistance. But, not long after they had arrived, he had a heart attack and died. It had happened whilst he was attending to some business on a very hot day, on the foreshore in Cape Town. It was all so very sudden that we put it down to the terrible stress of moving at their time of life!

I was really amazed at how the news affected me. I had spoken to him on many occasions about receiving the Lord Jesus as his Saviour but as far as I was aware he had never made his peace with God. I was shocked and deeply saddened and immediately made plans to attend his funeral in Cape Town.

I travelled on my own to Cape Town by plane, a

journey of around 1,300 miles. But in order to get the cheapest flight possible, I had to spend ten days or more in South Africa. My mother asked me to say a few words at his funeral, but once again a minister, this time a Church of England vicar was not keen on me participating. Yet, Despite that, I did say a few words honouring the man who had taken me in as a teenager and provided for me and my sister until we were able to provide for ourselves. He may have been a difficult man but I owe a lot to him and I thanked God for all that he did for me.

As I had to travel through Johannesburg, before catching my flight on to Bulawayo and home, I arranged to stay the weekend in the area with my brother Osmond and his wife Colleen. It seemed to be the ideal opportunity to attend a very successful church not far from where they were living. But, as my brother was not a church goer and lived out in the countryside, unless he gave me a lift I would not be going.

So, on the Saturday evening I asked my brother whether he would take me to the Rhema Bible Church in Randburg the following morning. He agreed to take me and praise God, he knew where the church was situated. It was not far from where he lived and as it is a very big building it is hard to miss. Because I had heard that it was very well attended, I suggested that we go early. We arrived in plenty of time and the huge auditorium, which seated several thousand, was almost empty. As we took our seats my brother looked around and asked in a tone of disbelief, **"Do you think that this place will fill up?"**

I must admit that it did not look very likely, but from what I had heard the place would be full before the meeting began and so I replied, **"I believe so. I have been told that it is always full."**

Within minutes people poured into the building and before long it was packed. They had a good music group and the praise and worship was great but, I was disappointed with the preaching. The ministry of the Word had very little substance, yet, when the appeal was made many people responded for prayer. The minister, Ray McCauley, had an evangelistic ministry and God was using him to bring people to Himself.

As we got up to leave and join the crowds heading for the door, I was surprised to discover that many in the congregation knew me and greeted me. There were many ex- Rhodesians (Zimbabweans) present who I knew, so much so that before we got to the door my brother jokingly turned to me and said, **"I know absolutely nobody here, but if we go to one of the local bars you will discover that I am also very well known!"**

I was thrilled that my brother had come with me that morning but was disappointed that the message was rather lacking in substance. But there was nothing more to be done, the next day I was on my way home to Bulawayo.

I was really looking forward to getting home and being with Mally and the boys after being away for ten days. However, when I arrived home, I was rather disappointed to discover that we had visitors. A family from church were staying with us for a few days before moving permanently down to South Africa. My very hospitable wife had invited them to stay as they had sold their house and were just waiting for their papers to clear before leaving. It was great to be home but to be quite honest I just wanted to be with my wife and family, and sadly, I was not the host that I ought to have been at that time.

MY MOTHER VISITS BULAWAYO.

It must have been sometime after the death of my step father that we arranged for my mother to visit us in Bulawayo. She had lived for the best part of thirty years in Bulawayo and there were a number of friends and relatives who still lived in the city that she wanted to visit. We did our best to make contact with as many as we could and arranged for her to visit them.

Among the people that we visited were relatives and others that we had known when I was a young boy growing up in Bulawayo. It was lovely to make contact again after so many years but sadly one of the ladies that we visited had major problems. These problems were largely due to the way that she had lived her life apart from the Lord. I tried to provide good Christian counsel but the problems were so complex that at the end I was quite exhausted.

Around the same time, I was asked to counsel to another lady unrelated to our family. Her problems were also amazingly complex. Once again, I went away completely exhausted. The reason that I am sharing these two stories is that SIN COMPLICATES our lives. If we want peace, joy, love and contentment in life we need to get back to God. He is the only one who can deliver us from the mess that we often make of our own lives. The Lord Jesus came specifically to bring 'sinners' to Himself and He alone is the answer to our need. If your life is a mess, cry out to the Lord in repentance as He is able to save you!!

My wife, Mally, could not have done more to care for my mother and we even discussed the possibility of bringing her back to Zimbabwe to stay with us. However, my Aunt Diana, my mother's youngest sister must have heard about it in England because she phoned me and said, **"Alan you must not take your mother back to Zimbabwe. She is much better off in every way in Cape Town in South Africa."**

Although I wanted to be a good son and a blessing to my mother, it was not very easy to know what we could do. We were living in Zimbabwe, my sister was in Canada, my eldest brother was in England, and my other brother, her nearest blood relative, was living outside Johannesburg, 1000 miles away from Cape Town. Although we discussed bringing her back to live with us in Zimbabwe, we never considered it as being viable. We knew that we would be leaving Zimbabwe, but not when, our future was far too uncertain for my mother to return to live with us!

It was lovely to have my mother visit, but it was soon time for her to return to Cape Town. Following his father's death, my stepbrother, Malcolm, and his wife Maureen, had been taking care of my mother, for which we were very grateful. As previously mentioned, she was living in the 'granny flat' attached to their house but, it was clear that they would not be able to look after her indefinitely. She was suffering from Parkinson's disease, and before his unexpected death, uncle Fred had been caring for her. As a result, not long after my stepfather's death my mother moved into the

Bay View Residential Home in Muizenberg which became her home until her death in 1989.

WEDDINGS.

While ministering in Kwe Kwe I had investigated what I needed to do to become a Marriage Officer. I soon discovered that it was not automatic for ministers to be licensed by the Government to legally perform weddings. I was told that it had been discovered, some years before, that there were more 'Marriage Officers' in the country than the number of marriages being performed every year. The reason for this state of affairs was that in addition to ministers and District Commissioners, there were many others who were legally able to perform weddings. As a result, the situation had changed, and each church denomination or movement was allocated sufficient Marriage Officers to meet their anticipated need. When I was the minister of the Kwe Kwe Assembly, it was not considered necessary for me to be a marriage Officer, however, that had changed by the time I arrived in Bulawayo.

During the first few months that I was in Bulawayo, Neil Gibbs was required to travel down to Bulawayo from Harare to officiate at weddings on at least two occasions. On one occasion, I saw him filling in the Marriage Register, while the Congregation were already gathering in the church. This is of course normally something that is done some time before the wedding. This was not because he had forgotten, or because he was ill prepared, but rather because he had so much on his plate.

NEIL GIBBS AND ALAN (AB)

It was clear that Bethshan was a much bigger fellowship than the other Assemblies where I had ministered. As a result, I would be required to conduct weddings for my own congregation, in addition to requests from others as well.

For example, on one occasion I was asked to conduct a wedding for a 'coloured' or mixed race couple, who were not members of our congregation. I was not a recognised Marriage Officer at the time and asked the Pastor of the Full Gospel Church to assist with the legal work. He was a lovely brother and willingly agreed to assist me, but his son was involved in some sporting activity that afternoon which he promised to go and watch. I said that we should be finished long before he was required to be at his son's event as the wedding was at least a couple of hours before he needed to be there. Sadly, I was really embarrassed, and it is possible that my friend missed his son's event as the bride finally showed up well over an hour late!

Well, to be quite honest, it was worth waiting for as I have never seen such a wedding party! The bride was beautiful, and her bridesmaids, were equally stunning, and there were more of them than I had ever seen at any other wedding. The groom was meticulously attired and his best man and groom's man equally well turned out. In addition, there were page boys, and flower girls, all beautifully dressed. It was without doubt a splendid affair.

Yet, as I began to conduct the wedding service and looked down at this amazing scene from the pulpit, there was one person who caught my eye. To be quite honest, I have never seen anything like it before or since. In fact, when you read what I am about to say, it is quite possibly that you will say, **"No, surely not. I cannot believe that!"**

Well, it is absolutely true! That special day, when everyone was meticulously attired, I spotted one lady who was not! Sitting on the back row was a lady with curlers in her hair! For the life of me I cannot imagine that she was going to attend a more important event than the event that she was attending right at that moment and yet she had curlers in her hair and a 'doek' (something like a shower cap) over the lot. Can you believe that?

Now, in order to become a recognised Marriage Officer I was required to study the Marriage Act and pass an exam. As the Full Gospel Minister had recently taken the exam and passed, I asked my friend to assist me. He was a great blessing and with his assistance it was not long before I had also passed the exam and was recognised as a Marriage Officer.

Over the coming years I discovered that when I took a wedding for someone from the 'white' tribe the bride could usually be expected to be about five minutes late and not much more. Then if the wedding was for someone from the 'coloured' tribe, as we have seen, it could be an hour late or possibly even longer. However, when I was asked to take a wedding for one of the 'black' tribe the conversation would go something like this.

I would say, **"Yes, I will be happy to take the wedding. When is it and what time is it due to take place?"**

The Enquirer would reply, **"The wedding will take place on Saturday ---------- at 10.00 am."**

"OK, so what time should I be there?" I would ask?

"Well we do not expect you at 10.00am, if you arrive at 11.00am that should be fine," they would say.

I was delighted to be able to take these weddings! They were always lovely occasions and it enabled me to learn a lot about the different people who made up the wonderful country in which I had been born. But I learned from experience, that even though the wedding was scheduled for 10.00 am and I had been told not to arrive before 11.00 am the chances of it taking place before 12.00 pm would be very slim. Yet, although that was the norm, as you will find out later, on one occasion I was nearly caught out when the bride and groom actually arrived on time, but that was when I was in Harare.

I usually did not attend the 'reception' unless I knew the couple particularly well, even though I was usually invited. However, on one occasion most likely when we were living in Harare, I was asked to take a wedding in one of the Tribal areas and because it was some distance from town, I agreed to attend the 'reception' and stay for part of the celebrations. On this occasion part of the 'reception' included raising a bit of extra money for the newlyweds but I did not really understand what was going on until much later.

We were enjoying the celebrations when I was asked by someone from the congregation to sing a song which came as a bit of a surprise. I had not been asked to sing at a wedding since I was in Chipinge, where I had been asked to sing in Afrikaans, and I thought that my 'wedding singing' days were now over. I was really impressed to be asked to sing, and stood up and burst into song. But I had barely sung one verse when I was told to stop. I was a bit confused but learned that someone had PAID FOR ME TO STOP! Sadly, they were more interested in raising money for the bride and groom than listening to me sing, and that well and truly brought my 'wedding singing' career to an end!

Whilst writing this book, I was contacted by Mark Kingham and asked if I would do a 'Renewal of Vows' service for his wife Yvonne and himself on the 1st of August 2021. This would be the fortieth anniversary of the day that I performed their wedding in Bulawayo at Bethshan. Theirs was one of a number of weddings at Bethshan that I had the privilege of conducting.

Apparently, Stan Smith, Mark's uncle, came back to the Lord as a result of attending their wedding. Prior to that he had not attended Church for 15 years. Praise God for such wonderful stories and I am very grateful to Mark for reminding me of these events.

Mark had been leading the youth when we

arrived in Bulawayo and I remember his concern for the young people when he informed me of his intention to move down to South Africa. He also reminded me of an event that had taken place at a youth meeting one Friday night. However, although I remember hearing about the event it had involved Paddy McCoun and not myself.

On that particular evening, Paddy was dressed as a 'hobo' or homeless man as part of the programme. Sadly, there was a bit of a disturbance outside and neighbours called the police. As a result, Paddy went outside and still dressed as a 'hobo' he addressed the police officer and said, **"Good evening officer, is there a problem? We are in the process of having a youth meeting and I am the minister ------."**

There is no doubt that youth meetings do have some memorable events and this was surely one of them!

BELLEVIEW ASSEMBLY & BETHSHAN TABERNACLE AMALGAMATE.

While ministering at Bethshan in Bulawayo, I was really blessed by Craig and Georgie Friend who were at that time ministering in Kadoma and Gary and Sharon Smith who were in Kwe Kwe. Both couples had family in Bulawayo and had been members of Bethshan before going into the Ministry. What impressed me and really blessed both Mally and I was that when they came to Bulawayo both Craig and Gary always made a point of paying us a visit. They did not need to do so, as I was well aware of the fact that they had family in Bulawayo, but it was a courtesy visit and it was very much appreciated by ourselves. Thank you, my dear friends, for honouring me with those visits, it meant a lot to us!

THE FAMILY 1981

Despite the closure of the 6th Avenue Assembly some time before we arrived in Bulawayo, there were now four functioning Assemblies in Bulawayo who were part of the group working with John Bond. Of these, the biggest and oldest was Bethshan where I was now the minister. Then there was Bulawayo North with Andy Murlis, followed by Belleview with Geoff Gonifas, and finally Calvary Chapel with Tom Nash who was pastoring the Assembly that he had pioneered not long before.

But, the change of government had unsettled many people who were now planning to leave. Before I moved to Bulawayo as so many were leaving the country it had been agreed to close Calvary Chapel. The remaining congregation moved to Bethshan and while he was still in the country Tom became Associate Minister, and Terry Tirrell, an Elder at Calvary Chapel, retained his status. Despite a few problems God was good to us and the 'amalgamation' of the two congregations went very well.

As we had got on so well it was great to be able to have some quality time with Geoff and Di Gonifas and their family as we were now labouring in the same city. Our sons were of a similar age and so it was great to get together. They were a real blessing to all of us.

On one occasion we were in the town when Geoff gave me a gift of Z$100.00. Our conversation went like this, **"Geoff, I cannot accept this from you, your need is as great or more than mine,"** I said.

Geoff said, **"AB, the Lord has put it on my heart to bless you and if I do not do it, I will lose out on the blessing that he has for me. You MUST take it or I will not be blessed!"**

Although I was not keen to do so, I had to put it in my wallet and keep quiet.

As I have already explained, many people were leaving the country. Because the congregation at Belleview was smaller, it was therefore more vulnerable than the one at Bethshan. One day Geoff came around to visit. He was really upset and said, **"I am sure that Peter and Sally and their family are planning to leave the fellowship."**

I knew Peter and Sally Davis very well as they had been saved some years before when we were in Kwe Kwe and so I said, **"How do you know? Have they said anything?"**

Geoff replied, **"No they have not said anything,**

I just know!"

After Geoff left, I gave Peter and Sally a ring and asked whether they were making plans to leave Belleview? When they assured me that they had no intention of leaving at that time, I asked them to let Geoff know which they promised to do. An hour or so later the phone rang and it was Geoff, **"Hi AB, it is just as I said! Peter and Sally are going to leave! They have asked to come round and see us and I know what they are going to say."**

I said, **"Hi Geoff, did Peter and Sally say why they wanted to come and see you?"**

"No," Geoff said, **"They just asked if they could come round and see us."**

I advised, **"Well, do not make any prior judgement, wait until they come round. They may be coming to see you about something entirely different. Just wait and see what they have to say."**

He then hung up, but sometime later the phone rang again and it was Geoff, **"Why did you not tell me why Peter and Sally were coming round to see me? You knew all the time!"**

I have not included this story to embarrass my friend but to warn us all of the danger of judging things before the time. We need to trust our God and let Him work things out for us. He knows what is taking place and we ought to just trust Him no matter what!

We were blessed to have a good relationship with Geoff and Di and their family which continues to the present day. However, the building they were using in Belleview had originally been built as a Nursery School. Due to changes in the population, the Nursery School had closed down some time before and the Assembly were able to acquire the building and use it as a church. Now, once again, things were changing radically, and sometime early in 1981, Geoff was told by the Deputy Minister of Education that unless the church started a Nursery School the Government would confiscate the building.

In discussion with Geoffrey Mkwanasi, it was agreed to transfer the building into the care and control of the Assemblies under Nicholas Bhengu. The congregation of the existing Belleview Assembly would link up with Bethshan and Geoff would become my Associate Pastor. In addition, a Nursery school led by an African American lady who was a missionary in Zimbabwe was started to satisfy the demands of the Ministry of Education and a new Assembly was established.

Sometime later, Terry and Tina Tirrell started a Junior Youth Group at Bethshan, which was composed almost exclusively of boys. Among the boys was our son, Mark, and Stephen and Jonathan Gonifas and they all had a great time. Our son, Matthew, was quite indignant as he was not allowed to attend until he started school.

THE CHURCH TREASURER.

Now, there is no doubt that whatever organisation we are part of, the Accountant, Book Keeper, or Treasurer is a very important position. It is of course the same in the church and one of the most necessary positions in any Assembly has to be the Treasurer. It is always very important that a faithful, honest, and reliable person is chosen for this role. Over the years in the different churches where I have ministered, we have had some exceptional people occupying this important position and I praise God for their faithfulness. Nevertheless, the person should really be referred to as the 'BOOK KEEPER' and not the TREASURER. Their job is not to CONTROL the money but to faithfully dispense it as decided by the Business Meeting of the fellowship and instructed by the Oversight of the Assembly which includes the Minister and Elders.

While we were at Bethshan we had a number of treasurers, but one person proved to be quite difficult. It seemed that he did not feel that he should 'GO AND PAY the MINISTER' but rather that the MINISTER should COME TO HIM for his pay. Sadly, during his time as our Treasurer he made me feel as if he was my boss, and I was required to stand in line and wait until he chose to pay me. It was really quite difficult!

Let me make it quite clear that if you occupy that position in your fellowship, remember that your minister is a GIFT FROM GOD to your local Church. He is not better than you, but he is GOD'S GIFT to you, so treat him as such!

"----- He gave gifts to men. -------And He Himself gave some to be apostles, some prophets, some evangelists, and some pastors and teachers, ---." Ephesians 4.8,11

As I have said, I have had some amazing people who have served faithfully, honestly, and reliably, in this role over the years, and I honour them, as what they do is often a thankless task. However, I have also had people who made me feel as if I was begging for my wages! Remember, what the Lord Jesus said,

"---- the labourer is worthy of his wages. ----." Luke 10.7

MISSION TO INDIA.

Moving on from there our next story takes us from Bulawayo all the way to India!

After a very successful 'mission' to India in 1981, Neil Gibbs was invited to return the following year. As a result, a team of 14 people were chosen to accompany him on a second 'mission' in January-February 1982. The team included Neil Gibbs and Paddy McCoun who were to concentrate on Evangelism. Then there was Mike Howard and Rodney Hein who were called upon to concentrate on praying for the sick; and lastly AB Robertson who was to concentrate on Teaching. In addition, there was Mally Robertson and Tim King and the Phileo music Group from Gweru. The music group were an enormous hit with the Indian people and included Abie and Laura Smit, Gilbert Evans, Urban and Dagma Smythe, and Sticks and Mary La Grange. Just to round things off, Neil asked me to bring along my piano accordion which proved easier said than done.

I would have had to go on my own but for the kindness of Rob and Fran Gordon who volunteered to look after our sons so that Mally could accompany me. Our sons were all quite young and so it was really difficult to leave them, but we were blessed to have this lovely couple look after them. The following was a report that I wrote about the trip, which was used to publicise the next Mission to India in 1983.

INDIA 1982.

Both Mally and I have considered it a great privilege to be part of the team that went to India this year. Without a doubt our lives can never be quite the same again.

There was poverty, the beggars, the busy millions all doing their best to survive. There was Bombay, a huge city, the commercial capital of the land, boasting around 30,000 taxis which were driven most dangerously, with hooters blowing continuously. Our eyes took in sights that stunned us, like thousands living on the streets and tens of thousands living in shanties.

We went south to another City and then to the southernmost tip of India to Cape Commeran. Hindu temples abound and the land is in need of the Saviour. In Southern India over 20% of the population are nominal Christians and huge churches vie with Hindu Temples. The Apostle Thomas came with the Gospel to these parts centuries ago, but India needs another Thomas today.

We preached, in a relatively new church in Bombay, to around 100 every night helping to establish a strong work for God in a new church. We preached to hungry souls of about 8,000 in the South and saw a real move of God's Spirit, with stories right out of the book of Acts. We then preached in a Crusade which ended up being very much an inter-church crusade and were given the opportunity on the Sunday of preaching to two big 'Church of South India' congregations one with

800 present and the other with 2-3000.

It is of course not possible, in a few weeks, to reach a great nation for Jesus, but by God's grace we have, we believe, assisted the local church in the great task of evangelism. It was thrilling to see hundreds come out for Jesus, to see bodies healed and demons cast out in Jesus' name. It was a most wonderful experience to see each one in the team play their part for the Lord Jesus.

We believe that God has opened a door for us. Let us hear the cry of India and continue to help in the evangelisation of India. Yours, in Jesus lovely name.

A.B. and Mally Robertson (Bulawayo A.O.G. Minister)

I am not too sure what we expected, however, nothing could have prepared us for the sights, sounds, and smells of India. The sheer number of people was something that was a little overwhelming. Travelling by car was a real experience as the driver seldom, if ever, stopped blowing his hooter. I explained to our driver that in Bulawayo you would be arrested if you drove like that, however, he replied that in Bombay you would soon be dead if you stopped blowing the horn.

Travelling on the trains was another experience. The train would arrive completely full but we would be told to get on board, and we would push our way on or we would never get to our destination. It was terrible seeing the many thousands of people living on the streets, some lived and died on the streets never having any other home, and the shanty towns were another eye opener. Among the sights that we saw were 'snake charmers' and many different businesses operating out in the open upon the streets of Bombay.

While in Bombay we were really privileged to spend a few nights at the Methodist Mission. It was a real sanctuary and we loved it there. However, Mally and I ended up at the YMCA after only two or three nights, as other people were booked into the Mission house and they were unable to accommodate us all.

Our new accommodation was also very good but when we looked around for the shower block we could not find any "Ladies" facilities on the floor where we were staying. This was not all that surprising as we were after all in the YMCA and we came to the conclusion that there were no 'Ladies' facilities but were perplexed that we had been given accommodation there. As a result, it was a bit awkward, and I had to stand guard whenever Mally needed to have a shower. But, on the last day, instead of using the lift, we happened to go down the stairs and, on the floor, below ours, what did we find, but a "LADIES SHOWER ROOM!" Maybe we should have asked!

While in Bombay, we went to the Taj Mahal Hotel and had a nice cup of tea, anything else was quite out of our reach. It was a fabulous hotel and a visit to the Gents or Ladies was an experience in itself. We discovered that there was a man (woman) holding hot towels for you, in order to wash your hands before leaving the facilities. Another experience that we were very privileged to enjoy was a swim at Beach Candy. The very best swimming pool in which I have ever enjoyed a swim. It was situated at what had been the Officers' Club when the British ruled India. How Neil Gibbs got us in there I will never know, but it was absolutely wonderful.

The contacts that Neil had in India had arranged three different 'Crusades' for us in different parts of that vast country. After a very successful week in Bombay, we were looking forward to a night off as we were all quite exhausted. We flew to Trivandrum in the South of India and were picked up at the airport by a Christian brother in a mini bus who took us to the Hotel where we were staying. But our driver then informed us that we did not have much time as we needed to leave for the meeting within the hour. This was news to all of us and so Neil said, **"But it was definitely arranged that we would have a night off before starting the next Crusade, so how come there is a meeting tonight?"**

The man replied that whatever arrangements had been made, we must come to the meeting that night! He explained that as we spoke, the people would already be starting to gather for the meeting at Karungal that evening. After some discussion it was agreed that I would go as the preacher, supported by Mike Howard and Rodney Hein. Just before we left Rodney asked the driver how far it was to the meeting? When the driver told him, he said, **"If I was driving, we would not have to leave so soon. It cannot take so long to travel so few miles?"**

He made that remark some time before we saw the traffic on the road. The road was crammed full of pedestrians by the thousands. In addition, there were cars, lorries, bicycles, ox carts and animals for the entire journey and we only just made it with a few minutes to spare. When we finally arrived, the people were there by the hundreds exactly as our driver had said. In fact, most nights the meetings were attended by around

8,000 people.

One thing that surprised us was that there were almost no 'seats.' The people were happy to sit on the ground of this market place, for hours at a time, every evening. The organisers had erected a platform which had a few seats for the visiting team, from where the musicians and the preacher would minister. The platform and the whole area where the people were sitting was very well illuminated with florescent lights.

Despite the confusion, relating to having a 'night off,' we praised God for the success of the first night of the second crusade. We were thrilled because a number of people came to Christ and wonderful miracles of healing took place. When we returned with our report to the hotel late that night, the rest of the team were very excited, and could hardly wait for the meeting the following night. On the second night even more people responded to the Gospel and the Lord 'confirmed His Word' with mighty miracles of healing and deliverance.

Sadly, I was not there the following night to witness what happened, as I stayed behind to have an evening off with Mally. After the team left, we went for a lovely walk along the sea shore. It was great to paddle in the sea and feel the sand beneath our feet, as Zimbabwe, as you know is an inland country with no seashore. Yet, we were both missing home, and one week without our sons was almost too much for us to handle. In addition, although we loved the Indian people, after one week away from home we would have loved to have seen a real 'black' African. In fact, the more we walked along the beach, that late afternoon, the more we missed our family and our home.

At that point, a man appeared and showed us a lot of shells, which we presumed he wanted to sell. We indicated that we had no desire to purchase them, and even if we did, we had very little 'foreign currency' and had to spend our few 'dollars' wisely. Sadly, millions of people in India are trying desperately to earn a living and we were approached constantly by people wanting to sell us something, and after just one week we were thoroughly tired of it.

I then decided to try and speak to him about the Lord Jesus; however, I had no Hindi, and he had no English which are the two official languages of the nation. To make things even more interesting, in addition to the two 'official languages' the nation recognises a further 22 languages and on the Indian sub-continent there are many hundreds of languages spoken by ordinary people.

As we could not communicate in either of the 'official languages' or any of the hundreds of other languages that are spoken in India I tried another tactic. I said a word that has not been translated from Hebrew into English nor into other languages in other translations of the Bible. The word that I said was 'HALLELUJAH!'

When I said, 'HALLELUJAH' his face lit up and he replied, 'HALLELUJAH' and we felt that we had met up with a believer. At that moment we came upon a ruined building on the beach which had been destroyed by the encroaching sea. We sat down on one of the remaining walls and when we began to pray, he joined us in prayer. By the time we finished our prayer and praise meeting with this Indian man our 'depression' had gone and we were rejoicing in the Lord. No sooner had we finished he excused himself, said goodbye, and went his way. I turned to Mally and said, **"When we get back to Zimbabwe, if we never get a letter from this man asking for financial help, we will know for certain that we have walked and talked with an angel of God today."**

We never met up with him again and we never heard from him in Zimbabwe, as far as we know. Was he really an 'angel' sent by God? We will never know this side of heaven; however, it was amazing how this encounter lifted our spirits and at the end of the three-week mission we even talked about returning as Missionaries to India!

The week passed by very quickly, filled with amazing stories of what God accomplished. At the end of our week's Crusade, we were informed by the organisers, that some very well-known foreign Evangelists had held Crusades in Karungal but, they had never had a response like they had seen that week. It seems that God had truly been at work.

The final week of our India Mission was held on the very tip of the Indian sub-continent in Kanniyakumari or Cape Comorin. We were accommodated at a place where we were informed, the British Governor of India had stayed many years before. When we were shown to our room, we discovered that the bed had a sheet on top, but nothing else. It was VERY HOT, but we were not used to having NOTHING on top of us and went to the desk to seek help. We ended up with what looked like a table cloth but whether we used it or not I cannot remember.

THE TEAM
(Neil and Paddy are missing)

The original site for the Crusade at Kanniyakumari had been vandalised by Hindu extremists before our arrival. As a result, the venue had been moved onto the property of Christ Church in Nagercoil. This church was part of the 'Church of South India', and they graciously allowed us to use their extensive grounds. Their large congregation gathered in a temporary building while a new Church building was being constructed.

Each of the Crusades had been conducted in very much the same way, with singing led by a local worship group before we were asked to take over. Our part of the service began with the Phileo Singing Group presenting a number of items, which were always well received. When they had finished, I would get up to bring TEACHING to the congregation for around 20 minutes. Then after I was finished, Neil or Paddy took over and PREACHED for around 20 minutes before making an appeal. This was then followed by caring for new converts, with Mike and Rod concentrating on praying for the sick.

Despite this rather lengthy programme, after we had been there for two or three nights we received a written message which read something like this, **"Dear Sirs, We represent the people who live in the houses surrounding the Crusade site and we have a request to make. Would both preachers please preach longer messages. Thank you."**

As I have explained, the meeting already lasted for possibly two hours, that was before we prayed for the sick, and yet we were asked to PREACH FOR LONGER! Such was the hunger we encountered in India!

On our last Sunday morning in India, we split up and attended different services. Most of the group accompanied Neil who preached at a large 'Assembly of God' Church in the area. Paddy was invited to preach at the largest 'Church of South India' congregation in the area, with a congregation of 2-3,000 people. Finally, I was privileged to address the congregation that met on site. Mally and I were very well received and they took photos of us with the leaders of the congregation which were then forwarded to us in Zimbabwe. That morning there were around eight hundred people present and we were thrilled that God had given us such wonderful opportunities.

Hallelujah!

Church Leaders, The Thatched Church & The New Church.

While we were in the area, Neil arranged for us to visit Kovalan beach. There were fishing boats at one end of the beach, but the other end was reserved for holiday makers. It was a fabulous beach, and the sea was lovely and warm and we hired a couple of boats and had a great time. As Mally and I were passing Neil's little boat, he made the following remark, **"At least while we are in the water no one will come up and want to sell us anything."**

He had hardly finished speaking, when a boat

drew near and a voice called out, **"Shells, cheap price!"**

It was hard to get away from the salesmen, as it seemed that they even followed us in little boats, however, as a result of Neil's comments, we all had a good laugh! Those few hours spent on the beach were a real blessing, and without doubt the beach was possibly the best that I have ever been to, and it was in the South of India.

It was soon time to return home, and although we were looking forward to seeing our three boys we were sad to leave India. We had some amazing memories of our three weeks on the Indian Sub-Continent. But we had a surprise awaiting us, as we were not going to leave on schedule!

On arrival at the airport, we were told that our flight home had been cancelled, and the next flight to Harare would not be leaving for a couple of days. After some discussion, Air India reluctantly agreed to provide us with accommodation in Bombay until they could fly us home.

We were provided with accommodation in a lovely Hotel built around a central courtyard with all the windows facing inwards. The corridor ran all around the outside with views of the city and the poverty beyond. Inside the hotel restaurants catered for all sorts of different tastes. We were able to visit some of them using the food vouchers provided by Air India. It was a wonderful gift from God and we all enjoyed the unexpected luxury. But, although it was a real blessing, praise God, we were soon on our way home to Bulawayo and to our family.

It was wonderful to be greeted by the 'smells' of Africa when we finally arrived home. It was also wonderful to see the lovely smiling faces of Africa! Praise God for HOME!

AN AMAZING CONVERT.

Having seen what the Lord did during our three weeks in India, it was wonderful to know that the Lord was at work in Bulawayo as well. One Sunday evening as an example, Gary Trevor was accompanied by a Woman Police Officer when on duty with the "A" Reserve of the police force. As was his normal practice, when on duty on Sunday evening, he took his 'lunch break' when the service was being held at Bethshan. On this particular evening, he parked his Patrol Car outside the Assembly and the WPO accompanied him into the service. When they arrived, I had already started preaching but I was pleasantly surprised when she responded to the appeal at the close of the service.

After the morning service a couple of weeks later, I gave her a lift home. She lived on the other side of Bulawayo, some distance beyond where I had grown up as a child. On the way, I spoke to her about the importance of being 'baptised by immersion' if she was serious about following the Lord Jesus. As it turned out, she was only too keen to be baptised, and so we arranged for the baptism to take place the following Sunday evening. I explained that she would be required to give a testimony on how she had come to know the Lord Jesus as her Saviour before being baptised. I made it clear that it could be a short public testimony or a long testimony depending on how she felt about speaking in public. With no hesitation she replied that her testimony would be quite long.

As a result, before being baptised, the following Sunday evening, she gave her testimony to the gathered congregation. As part of a fairly long testimony, she said something like the following,

"During the 'bush war' I joined up with the 'freedom fighters' as I believed they were fighting for the freedom of our people. I did not 'hate' the white man but wanted a change of government. However, one day we were involved in an engagement with the government forces and all my companions were killed except me. What I saw that day changed my thinking, as in that engagement all the soldiers who had been involved in killing my friends were 'white men.' As a result, from that day, I began to hate the 'white man'.

It is a miracle that I have come to know Jesus as my Saviour! It is even more of a miracle that I am being baptised by a 'white' man in a predominantly 'white' Church. I have accepted Jesus Christ as my Lord and Saviour and this evening I want to follow Him through the waters of baptism."

As the majority of the 'regulars' in the Rhodesian Army were 'black' soldiers it is quite likely that she had been involved with the Rhodesian Light Infantry (RLI) who were an all 'white' military unit. It must have been a difficult thing for her to see all of her 'comrades' killed, but it must have been the mercy of God that she survived. Hate is a terrible thing and it is only when we allow the Lord Jesus Christ to deal with us that we can be set free. Sadly, long after any war is over, many people never get over the loss of loved ones and friends and in addition, they allow hatred to fester and destroy their own lives as well.

What a testimony for us to hear at Bethshan!

When I had taken her home, the Sunday before, she had explained to me that her uncle was one of the members of the new government. His name was very well-known to all of us and he was considered a real radical and a very dangerous man. Shortly after she became a 'believer,' he paid her a visit at her home and spotted her Bible on her bedside table. When he asked her about the Bible, she told him what had happened, and how she had asked Jesus into her life. Praise God that the word of God was able to reach into the heart of the new government through the words of this new convert.

However, that was not all, when Jim McCay (someone from our congregation) and his family emigrated to Australia, this 'new believer's' uncle purchased their house. Later when he refurbished the house it was one of our 'members' who advised him on what furniture to purchase etc. If that was not enough, sometime after I left Bulawayo and moved back to Harare, I believe that he actually came to one of the meetings at Bethshan when Gary Smith was the minister. Who knows what God can do when He begins to work in the hearts of unbelievers? But if this man failed to turn to the Lord, it was not because the Lord had failed to reach out to him!

Sadly, sometime later we lost contact with this woman. I believe that it was possibly as a result of a rather unacceptable racist remark, that she overheard from one of the people in the congregation. I never knew all the details and was so sad that it had taken place. Sometime before, when some 'coloured people' that is people of mixed race, started attending

Bethshan, my good friend Neil Gibbs who was the minister at the time, said something like the following, **"If I hear any racially unacceptable comments from this congregation I am leaving."**

As I have already explained, I said something similar when I was in Kwe Kwe! But, in this case, sad to say, I do not remember saying anything, possibly because the damage was already done, and the woman had left. I do hope that this foolish comment never turned her away from Jesus as that would be terribly sad as her salvation was a complete miracle!

TWO VISITS TO CHIPINGE.

Having been away from Chipinge for some time, I decided that it was time to visit and made arrangements to do so. I had heard good reports about what Mike Howard was doing and how he had mobilised the whole congregation in an outreach to the wider community. Among other things, I heard stories about members of the congregation preaching to the soldiers of the new Zimbabwe Army at a base just outside Chipinge. In addition, Mike accompanied by Rod and Ellie Hein were going into Mozambique ministering to the poorest of the poor, and Kath Neville was travelling into the Tribal areas with a mobile clinic provided by Jimmy Swaggart Ministries. She was providing them with medical treatment as well as the Good News of the Gospel.

When we went to Chipinge, we stayed with Mike in the three bedroomed house that had been purchased when we were there. The outreach taking place all around Chipinge and beyond was really exciting, however, it appeared that no one was being added to the local church which was a bad sign. While we were there, Mike announced a special weekend of ministry with some visiting lady speaker and Mally was encouraged to attend with some of the ladies from Bethshan. Those that attended had a wonderful weekend and came back refreshed and uplifted. The following Sunday morning at Bethshan, all these ladies danced joyfully before the Lord during the Sunday morning service. Sadly, it was something Mally's husband was not all that pleased about at the time, which was a real pity. I was wrong, and should have encouraged my wife, as she had been truly blessed by her weekend away.

HOSPITAL VISITATION.

One day while I was with Geoff Gonifas at Bethshan he had a phone call. A lady who had been attending the services with her husband was in hospital dying of cancer and he asked us to visit his wife. As Mally was out in our car, we proceeded to the hospital in Geoff's car. Under normal circumstances that would not have been a problem, however, after having endless car problems, Geoff had scrapped his old car, and knowing of his predicament, one of the congregation offered to help. He offered to give him his old Fiat 500 which needed a respray amongst other things. Not wanting to receive it for nothing, Geoff asked him how much he wanted for the car. He was told that all he would accept in exchange was Geoff's wheelbarrow, as he needed a wheelbarrow. Geoff accepted the deal and decided to spruce up his new acquisition by giving it a respray. Sadly, on the day we went to the hospital together, all the paint had been scraped off the car in preparation for the new paint job. As you can imagine the car was not looking at its best!

We spent some time with the lady in hospital and decided to visit her husband on the way home. He was the top man at Duly's in Bulawayo, which before economic sanctions had been the main Ford Motor Car dealership in Rhodesia. As a result, for some years, they, like everyone else in the country, had sold whatever motor cars they could get. This man and his wife both owned almost new, Nissan Sunny motor cars, and lived in a lovely house in a very good neighbourhood.

We pulled up at the gate, left the car outside, and knocked at the door, and were made very welcome. We did not stay long, and after praying with the sick lady's husband, he saw us to the gate. After saying our goodbye's, sadly, the car would not start, and after Geoff had tried for a few minutes the gentleman said, **"Why not leave your car here, take my wife's car, and sort out your car in the morning?"**

But Geoff did not give up easily, and a few seconds later it burst into life and we waved goodbye. On the way home we drove past the home of a fellow minister who was the pastor of a rapidly growing church in the city. As we were going past, Geoff explained that this pastor also possessed an almost new, Nissan Sunny, and recently someone from his congregation had emigrated and presented an almost new, Nissan Sunny to his wife as a gift. He then said, **'I sometimes find it difficult to understand the Bible verse that states: - "---- that God is no respecter of**

persons ---."'

Although we both laughed heartily, I knew precisely what Geoff was saying. We both knew that it was not easy to understand the different experiences that people have to go through.

For example, why did some people have to struggle so much in life, and others seem to have things so easy? During the last few years, I had possessed 3 brand new motor cars when it was almost impossible to purchase new motor cars in Rhodesia/Zimbabwe, and my friend was trying to make do with the old car that we were travelling in that day. But after a good laugh, we arrived at my home where he dropped me off and then returned to his own family.

We need to remember what Jesus said to Peter, many years ago. The Lord told him that he would suffer for the cause of the Gospel, but when Peter saw John following them, he said, **'"But Lord, what about this man?" Jesus said to him, "If I will that he remain till I come, what is that to you? You follow Me."'** John **21.21-22**

So often we spend all of our time comparing ourselves with others, and forget that we are called to follow Jesus. The direction that He chooses for us and the type of life that we are called to live may be very different from that chosen by the Lord for some other man or woman of God. Just like Peter, The Lord calls out to us today to take our eyes off other people and get on with serving Him, when he says, **'"--- what is that to you? You follow Me."'** John **21.21-22**

My friend Geoff had a real 'pastor's' heart and also tended to be more of an evangelist than myself. As we discussed the situation of the woman dying in hospital, I came to realise that Geoff was quite willing to stay all night at the hospital with a person who was dying and had done so on a number of occasions. I was just not like that and I honour him for being willing to stay with someone while they crossed over from life into death.

THE MUSIC MACHINE.

You never know what a day will bring forth and we were about to experience something wonderful at Bethshan. It began when I was approached by Wanda Anderson and asked whether she had my backing to produce a Children's, Christian Musical at Bethshan called 'THE MUSIC MACHINE.' It was a 'musical' that she produced in the church that she had attended when she was at Bible College in the USA. She was the daughter of the senior minister of the Full Gospel Church in Zimbabwe and she and her husband Dennis were in fellowship with us at Bethshan.

I was only too keen to give her my support and so she immediately set about arranging to produce this wonderful musical. But, if she was to succeed, it was clear from the start that it would require the backing of the whole Assembly. The musical was based on the 'Fruit of the Spirit' which Paul the apostle spoke about in his letter to the churches of Galatia. **Galatians 5.22-23**

The Music Machine was quite a production and around 40 children participated drawn from our Sunday Schools at Bethshan and Waterford. The main children's roles were played by Chad Warren who was STEVIE and Adele Robinson who was NANCY. The main adult role of THE CONDUCTOR was played by Geoff Gonifas. The different songs about the fruit of the

Spirit were sung by the following members of the congregation: -

PATIENCE was sung by Dennis Anderson, A.B. Robertson and Ian Brand with his deep bass voice.
GENTLENESS was sung by Dawn Brand.
JOY was sung by Sharon Blackmore, Terry Blackmore, Adelaide du Plessis, and Rose Whiting.
PEACE was sung by David Amyot, and Mark, and Matthew Robertson.
KINDNESS was sung by Sophie Sharp

The other songs, about LOVE, GOODNESS, FAITH, and SELF CONTROL were sung either by the CONDUCTOR as a solo, or supported by all the children. All the singers and especially the children did a marvelous job.

But that was not all, Dawn Brand made the costumes, art work was done by Carol Rowlands and Marie du Plessis, lighting was managed by Terry Tirrel, and Ian Brand organised the Music Machine itself. The music was provided by Gerry Amyot on the piano, Freddie Van Rensburg on the Guitar and the Violin, Christine Robinson on the tambourine, A.B. Robertson on the Piano accordion, and finally Ian Brand on the harmonica and the drums. Everyone did a marvelous job and Gerry Amyot was brilliant.

In December 1982, The Music Machine was performed at Bethshan, to a packed church. It was also put on in the Centenary Park where it was very well received, but that was not all! While we were rehearsing, Wanda asked me if she could approach the Zimbabwe Broadcasting Corporation with a view to producing it for Television. I must say that I was very skeptical as at the time we were far from perfect and things were changing very rapidly in Zimbabwe, however I told her to go ahead.

At the very next rehearsal, a representative of ZBC arrived to view the show. To my surprise, they agreed to record the Music Machine for TV and a day was set for us to travel to the studios to have it recorded. This naturally caused a lot of excitement for all of us as it was a wonderful opportunity to proclaim the Word of God on national Television to the entire viewing population. Once it was recorded, it was screened on two separate occasions from the Bulawayo studios and also shown to the rest of the viewing public in Zimbabwe from the Harare studios. It was a 'children's' musical and as such aimed at the younger viewing public but who knows how many people, adults and children were drawn closer to the Lord Jesus through this production? Praise God for the boldness of Wanda Anderson and for the commitment of all those involved. God is so good!

On the day that we went to the studio everyone was excited but, before facing the camera's it seemed that the preparations would never end. Much to my disgust they wanted to put powder on my face etc. so that my face would appear in a good light on TV. Although I resisted, I finally had to give in and allow them to do what they wanted to do. What people will do to appear on TV?

When we were all finally ready, filming commenced. The 40 or so children who represented both of our Sunday Schools, behaved exceptionally well. Those that had individual parts never faltered and when they all sang together it was wonderful. Sadly, it was at the studios that Mark had another attack, but he was very brave, and despite the pain he was able to continue to participate. The pain did finally settle down for which we praised God.

THE MUSIC MACHINE

I was amazed at Geoff, as he had the major singing role, and he performed without any difficulty having learned all his words perfectly. But there was one fly in the ointment and that was one of the men who sang the song PATIENCE. Yes, you have guessed it, I messed up singing my solo VERSE and it had to be filmed more than once before I got it right. Geoff had so many words to learn and I had only a few, and yet it was yours truly who messed up!

THE CHRISTMAS CANTATA.

Believe it or not, not long after we began to rehearse THE MUSIC MACHINE, which was a major production, involving the whole Assembly, Geraldine Amyot our chief musician, wanted to see me. She asked me whether I would agree to her producing a CHRISTMAS CANTATA at Bethshan that same year. Although I knew that it would be very demanding for all involved, I agreed to her going ahead largely because of her evident enthusiasm. What an amazing year, a CHRISTMAS CANTATA had never been produced at Bethshan and neither had a children's musical and yet the Lord was evidently in both productions!

The CHRISTMAS CANTATA was called JOY TO THE WORLD by John W. Peterson and was conducted by Geraldine Amyot. The pianist was Ann Whiting and the narrator was Graham Whiting one of our elders at the time. The choir included the following:-

FIRST SOPRANOS
Dawn Brand, Libby Channer, Dawn Pearmain, Christine Robinson, Carol Rowlands, Sophie Sharp.
SECOND SOPRANOS
Kerrie Dreyer, Greta de Bruyn, Elsie Goosen, Colleen Pearmain
ALTOS
Rose Blackmore, Dorothy Clarke, Danielle Dreyer, Francis Gordon, Yvonne Kingham,
Mally Robertson, Gladys Wood
TENORS
Gerald Clarke, Keven Geer, Geoff Gonifas, Percy Warren, David Whiting

BASSES
Ian Brand, A.B. Robertson, Freddy van Rensburg
SOLOISTS
Rose Blackmore, Christine Robinson, Geoff Gonifas,
A.B. Robertson, Percy Warren
LADIES SEXTET
Dawn Brand, Danielle Dreyer, Kerrie Dreyer, Fran
Gordon, Mally Robertson, Valerie Whiting

As I am typing this story, I am amazed at how many
people were involved in these two productions, in fact
it really involved the entire congregation in one way or
the other. Just like The MUSIC MACHINE, once the
CHRISTMAS CANTATA had been properly rehearsed
it was performed at different venues.

Naturally, we put it on at Bethshan for the local
congregation. However, the main performance took
place at a public hall in Bulawayo, which was packed
out for the performance. Then we took it to the mental
hospital in Bulawayo, where, I am sure, the patients
enjoyed the production. One thing is sure, and that is
that the staff were thrilled that we put on the Cantata
for them at INGUCHENI HOSPITAL and their
response really made our day.

As I look back on those two Musical productions,
produced during that amazing time, I cannot but thank
God that we were able to be part of it all. For that
particular season, the Lord brought together an
amazing group of incredibly talented people who were
willing to work together to produce two wonderful
musicals for the glory of God. The success of THE
MUSIC MACHINE, and THE CHRISTMAS CANTATA

was more than we could ever have hoped for. They were both produced in December 1982 but, the following year, we would not have been able to produce either production, as things were about to change significantly.

Among other things, Geoff Gonifas, our most important adult singer in The Music Machine, would soon leave Bulawayo as he, Diana and their family moved to Harare. In addition, Dennis and Wanda Anderson (the producer of The Music Machine) left us to take up a position in full time ministry with the Full Gospel Church. Sadly, Wanda was not to live long and a few years later she went home to be with the Lord. In addition to these dear people, within a short time, many others had moved away from Bulawayo, to other towns and countries. In addition, some left Bethshan to join other congregations in Bulawayo, including Geraldine Amyot our wonderful pianist, producer of the Cantata.

There can be no doubt that the Lord God brought together the right people at Bethshan in 1982 in order to produce those two wonderful productions! Praise His name! Sadly, although members of the congregation tried to get a copy of the video recording of THE MUSIC MACHINE from the ZBC, I do not know of anyone who was successful.

NEW RESPONSIBILITIES AHEAD.

The next trip to India was due to take place at the beginning of 1983 and once again Mally and I were to be part of the team. I was thrilled to discover that 'THE HARVEST TIME COUNTRY GOSPEL GROUP,' were going to accompany us to India. They had been such a blessing at the 'NOW IS THE HOUR' crusade that Neil Gibbs had staged in Chipinge. In preparation for the trip, we had already received our Cholera inoculations which were considered absolutely essential when travelling to India. It was then that we had a phone call from Neil Gibbs.

Neil started, **"Good afternoon AB I trust that you, Mally and the family are all well?"**

"Hi Neil," I replied, **"Yes, we are all very well thank you, and Mally and I are really looking forward to the upcoming Mission to India. How are you, Marge and the family?"**

"We are all well thank you," he said, **"However I have something disappointing to share with you. Sadly, I have to inform you that you and Mally will need to remain in Zimbabwe, and not travel to India on this occasion. There are some difficulties in Zimbabwe at present, and with me moving to South Africa as soon as I return, John Bond and I do not feel that it is a good idea for you to be out of the country at this time. So, you will have to remain at home in order to keep an eye on everything here."**

I was really disappointed, as was Mally when I told her, but after Neil explained to me what the problems were, I knew that I had to stay.

As mentioned by Neil in his conversation with me, he and Marge would be leaving for South Africa a few days after he returned from India. With Neil leaving, I had been asked to take his place as John Bond's representative in the country. The departure of Neil Gibbs for South Africa would be a real loss to the work in Zimbabwe and his shoes would be very difficult to fill. However, with the help of the Lord I was ready for the challenge as always. I could not do the job without His help but I knew that He would be with me!

But ----------, I cannot tell you how disappointed we were to miss out on a return trip to the Sub-Continent of India. What made it particularly difficult to take, was that we had already had our Cholera inoculations! We had suffered all that pain for nothing! However, despite our disappointment a new Chapter in our lives was now beginning!

Chapter 2

NATIONAL LEADERSHIP

A) BULAWAYO 1983

BETHSHAN TABERNACLE.

After taking over the leadership role from Neil Gibbs, I initially continued to also remain Senior Pastor of Bethshan Tabernacle in Bulawayo. However, my new role involved a fair bit of extra work because of all the added responsibilities. It is possible that I was no longer **'seen'** to be as committed to the work in Bulawayo as I had been previously and may well go some way to explain what took place that year.

Despite the great success achieved the previous year when the entire Assembly pulled together, it was soon apparent that all was not well at Bethshan. It came to my attention one Saturday morning when I called for a 'work party' to meet at the Church. I was really disappointed by the response; it was very discouraging! Nevertheless, as much needed to be done, I called for another 'work party' a couple of weeks later. Sadly, the response was even worse, but, when I commented on the poor turnout one of the elders said, **"If the people are being blessed, they will respond, so clearly they are not happy."**

To be quite honest, I could not figure out what could be wrong!

Around about that time, because our Sunday School facilities were inadequate, I suggested that we construct a block of classrooms outside the main building. During the ministry of Bill Mundell, a very nice toilet block, had been constructed at the rear of the building. I wanted to build an equally well constructed block of classrooms for the Sunday School. This of course would be expensive and there was some resistance to spending that type of money. We all agreed that we needed better Sunday School facilities and so someone suggested that we put up a 'prefab' building, which would be much cheaper. Although this was not my original idea, a 'prefab' building was constructed for the Sunday School, which later became known as,

"A.B's FOLLY."

It may still be known as that today, I repeat, it was **not** my idea!

To return to the unhappiness at Bethshan, and certain problems that we were later to experience, I believe they could well be related to a simple fact; WE WERE NO LONGER EXPANDING AS A MOVEMENT IN BULAWAYO!

For some years, before 1969, there were two Assemblies in Bulawayo, 6th Avenue and Bethshan Tabernacle, but, for various good reasons they decided to amalgamate. During the next few years under Bill Mundell's wonderful evangelistic ministry, Bethshan grew significantly. Then, in 1976, Bill left Bethshan in order to pioneer a new Assembly across town in Queens Park which became known as Bulawayo North. Then, having established a viable Assembly in Queens Park, he continued his evangelistic work by pioneering another Assembly at Belleview, on the West of the city, where he moved in early 1979.

In addition to the evangelistic and Church planting work of Bill Mundell, yet another Assembly opened in mid-1978. This Assembly, in the city centre, known as CALVARY CHAPEL, was established by Tom Nash, who had previously been an Elder at Bethshan. But things were changing rapidly and these four Assemblies had been reduced to two by 1983 and, later still, would once again become only one!

I believe this had a profound effect upon Bethshan and indeed upon the whole 'Assembly of God' work in Zimbabwe. The 'white' congregations were suddenly starting to close and instead of looking outward, which had always been our mission, we were now increasingly looking inward. As a result, we were bound to have a few problems. Although there were a few problems at Bethshan during the years that I was there, I have decided to only mention a couple. The reason that I mention the following story is that it is necessary to give some background to a city-wide Crusade that we held in Bulawayo in 1983.

It so happened that Paul Lange (South Africa) and Solomon Wasker (India), were due to visit Bethshan during the very same month that year. As the dates were so close, and they were both such accomplished men of God, I suggested to the Oversight that we have a city-wide crusade. In this case I suggested that we invite Bulawayo North AOG, the Full Gospel Church, and the Apostolic Faith Mission to join us in an eight-day crusade in the City Hall. Having presented my plan to the oversight at Bethshan and won their approval, I contacted the other ministers in town and was encouraged by their enthusiastic response.

When we met to make plans for the Crusade, it was decided that each fellowship would be responsible for a particular aspect of the meetings. For example, one Minister would be responsible for training the 'counsellors,' and another would be responsible for organising the 'ushers,' who would all be recruited from the participating congregations. Once that had been agreed, volunteers were requested to sign up for a short training session to be run by the person responsible.

Although we were sponsoring the crusade, I was determined that it would be a joint effort involving all the participating congregations. We made it clear from the start that this was being done for the extension of God's Kingdom and not primarily for any particular congregation. The response from all the participating churches was so positive that it looked like we would have a great crusade at the Bulawayo City Hall.

But, a short while before the meetings were to take place, I received a phone call from the minister organising the counsellors, followed by a phone call from the minister in charge of the ushers! They informed me that they had not received any names from Bethshan and requested them urgently, as there were only a few days left before the crusade. Having heard what they had to say, I was very disappointed but promised to let them know following the Sunday services.

It must have been on the Saturday that I had a phone call from an Australian man and our conversation went something like this, "I have seen your advert in the Newspaper," said the Aussie, "But it does not say 'ALL WELCOME' so I want to know whether I will be welcome."

"Of course, you will be welcome," I replied, "why on earth would we put an advert in the newspaper if we were not inviting people to attend?"

"OK, I just wanted to check. I will be there on Sunday," the Aussie stated.

I had really never heard anything quite so silly.

That Sunday morning, before we sang the closing hymn, I asked the congregation to remain seated and addressed the person responsible for taking the names of the volunteers for the Crusade, "----- the city-wide crusade is due to take place very soon and the Full Gospel Minister is in urgent need of the names of any volunteers. Would you tell us how many people have volunteered as counsellors for the Crusade?"

The person responsible replied, "Three!"

I exclaimed, "Only three! That is not acceptable! I understand that Bulawayo North have 10 people signed up as Counsellors and they are a much smaller fellowship than Bethshan."

I then addressed the congregation and said, "If you are willing to volunteer as a counsellor for the city-wide crusade would you please stand to your feet so that -------- can take your name."

I was amazed when nobody responded by standing to their feet, and so turning my attention once again to the person responsible for taking the names I continued, "Well, -----, how many names do you have of people who have volunteered to be ushers at the Crusade?"

"I have three names!" the person responded.

I said, "I cannot believe this! We are sponsoring this crusade, yet we only have 3 people volunteering to assist as ushers? Once again, I have been advised that Bulawayo North, a much smaller Assembly than ours, have 10 volunteers."

Feeling increasingly discouraged I once again turned my attention to the congregation and said, "If you are willing to assist as an usher in the Crusade, would you please stand to your feet so that ------- can take your name."

I was once again shocked when not one person stood to their feet and so after a few minutes I said, "We will sing the final hymn which is -----."

Once we had sung the hymn, I asked the congregation to be seated again and said, "This crusade is being put on by Bethshan! It was our suggestion! The speakers are both being provided by ourselves! Therefore, if this is how this congregation is prepared to back this important outreach in Bulawayo, then you can be sure that before the end of this year I will be leaving."

Having said that, I picked up my briefcase, walked out, went into my office near the entrance to the building, and most likely put my feet on my desk. I did not even close the meeting in prayer, I was so disappointed. However, once I had left, the person responsible for taking the names of the volunteers, rose to his feet and said, "The reason that no one is backing the crusade and volunteering to be counsellors or ushers is that this Assembly is very divided."

He may well have continued, but Graham Whiting, the senior Elder, and a lovely man of God, took charge, and told him to be seated, and closed the meeting in prayer.

Sadly, following that morning's meeting there were a few resignations, and a few people left Bethshan but, praise God, it was not really a 'split.'

However, before continuing to explain what happened at the crusade, let me tell you what happened to our Australian friend as he phoned again that Monday morning. He said, **"I arrived at your Church for the service in plenty of time on Sunday morning and walked up and down outside the Assembly a number of times before plucking up enough courage to enter the building as I have not been to Church for years. But, after having such a struggle to come to church, what did I find? I walked right into a 'split!' So, what I would like to know from you is, could you recommend another Church to me?"**

I really did feel sorry for the man, it had been a difficult meeting for everyone!

"My apologies, I am sorry that your first visit to Bethshan ended as it did. However, in answer to your question there are a number of good fellowships in Bulawayo that I would be happy to recommend. For example, there is the Bulawayo North AOG, the Full Gospel Church and the Apostolic Faith Mission, the Baptist Church, and many others."

After a short conversation with the man, I replaced the receiver. I am not sure whether he visited any of these churches but a week or two later he returned to Bethshan and from then on, he attended regularly.

What happened at Bethshan is sadly not unique. Just like any family, the 'church family,' will be faced with very difficult problems from time to time and they can be very upsetting. The Bible tells us that God's blessing rests upon congregations that walk in unity.

As a result, we need to be very careful to 'build' our local church, we must never be guilty of pulling it down! We need to always strive for unity in our local fellowship!

"Behold, how good and how pleasant it is for brethren to dwell together in unity! ------------For there the Lord commanded the blessing — life forevermore." Psalm 133.1,3

Well as unlikely as it may seem, the city-wide crusade took place as planned. In fact, in the end, Bethshan produced more counsellors and more ushers than any of the other congregations. In addition, as the City Hall did not have an adequate PA system, Phil D'Aguiar, someone from the congregation, took it upon himself to build a PA system from scratch for the occasion!

Solomon Wasker, our visitor from India, was very impressed when he realised that someone from our congregation had made the PA system from scratch. He had been involved in many crusades in India and informed us that it was the best that he had ever used. In fact, Bethshan excelled as only it was capable of doing for which I really praised God. Although there were not a large number of decisions for Christ, I believe that the members of the participating congregations, were all encouraged in their walk with the Lord!

CHILDREN, SCHOOLS AND TRAILERS.

Moving on from there, our children were getting older and at the beginning of 1983 it was time for our second son, Matthew, to start school. He was enrolled at

Hillside Infants School and Mark moved up to the Junior School. We were truly blessed to have this excellent Government School so close to where we were living.

Among the many who were leaving the country at that time, were Jim McCay and his family who were leaving for Australia. He came to see me with a proposition, he asked me if I was willing to do a swap, his very nice trailer for my Motorcycle. He wasn't planning to take his trailer with him but if he had a motorbike, it would enable him to have wheels when he arrived down under. At the time there were major restrictions on what you could and couldn't take with you when you left the country. In addition, anything that you took had to be a certain age or else you could not take it. When I explained that I hadn't finished paying for my bike he informed me that he was happy to pay off the debt in addition to providing me with a trailer. The agreement was struck, and as a result I became the proud owner of a trailer, but my lovely motorcycle joined the procession of those leaving the country.

PROBLEMS.

It was also in 1983, that Simon Rhodes joined me at Bethshan as my assistant after returning from Bible College in Wales. It was great to have them at Bethshan as, since we had lived in Chipinge, Simon, Rena and their son Adam had always been a great blessing to us.

In addition to getting a new assistant, I also took on a secretary due to my increased responsibilities, who proved to be a great help.

Nevertheless, not long after Simon came to Bethshan, a problem arose when a certain couple began to attend the Assembly. The man had been an elder in a local Church, but sadly he had destroyed his marriage by having an affair with a woman from another fellowship. The affair had begun when they both started attending an early morning prayer meeting held in a third church. As her home was not far from where he lived, he offered to give her a lift to the meetings in the mornings. Not long afterwards the relationship became anything but spiritual and led to his wife filing for divorce. He was no longer an Elder and they were understandably no longer attending their previous churches.

Before we proceed, let me make it perfectly clear that this couple sinned against God, their respective spouses, and their children. However, as an 'Elder' in his church, the man had done terrible harm not only to himself and his family, but also to those who had previously looked up to him. The faith of many would have been challenged by what he had done, and some would have turned away from their faith in the Lord as a result. We need to understand that if we are in leadership, we have a great responsibility. We dare not 'mess around' as the Lord is watching! In addition, our sinful actions will have a negative impact upon many people, Christians and unbelievers!

We need to remember that God hates sin, and He went to great lengths to SAVE us from our sins. The love that God has for us, was clearly revealed when He gave his SON to rescue us from SIN! No matter who we are, Ministers, Elders, Deacons, Sunday School

Superintendents, Youth Leaders and others, we will face many temptations during our lives. The problem is that whoever we are, at certain times we can be very vulnerable. In those times in particular, we need to take care not to foolishly expose ourselves to danger as the enemy of our souls longs to destroy us. The Word of God, which is our guide to life, has the following to say,

"Be sober, be vigilant; because your adversity the devil walks about like a roaring lion, seeking whom he may devour; resist him, steadfast in the faith, -----."
1 Peter 5.8-9a

When I discovered that this couple began attending Bethshan not long after it had all come into the open, I realised that we could not just sit back and do nothing! We had a major problem on our hands, and so I called a Ministers' and Elders' meeting to determine what we should do. I felt that it was vital that we deal with this particular issue as soon as possible, we could not just ignore it! Sadly, despite my efforts, which I will not go into at this time, the issue remained unresolved and so I called another meeting, this time with the leaders of the three Churches that had been affected by this couple's sin.

The meeting that night included the Ministers and Elders of the offending couple's former churches, and the Oversight of Bethshan. After a fair amount of discussion, they agreed almost unanimously with a plan which I believed was totally unrealistic. But a decision had to be made that evening as the couple were in the church, waiting to hear from us! As a result, I said, **"As this issue is urgent and needs to be**

70

resolved I will stand with you in what you propose. But, as I believe that what you are proposing will not work, one of you will need to tell the couple what you have decided. We can call them in and one of you will need to speak as I cannot. Despite this, I will stand with you in what you are proposing."

A spokesman was selected and the couple were called in and informed of the decision. I take no delight in saying that it turned out exactly as I had predicted. I was convinced that what was proposed was not going to work.

You may well have noticed how I responded to a decision that was contrary to what I believed. Although I disagreed and knew in my heart that it was unworkable, I was prepared to support the decision of the majority. As leaders of the work of God, we cannot always get what we want, but we need to stand together in unity as the work that we are involved in is so important. There are times when it is better to unite behind the majority, than cause division. At other times it may be so important that it is better to resign and quietly move away. That evening I decided to stand with the majority Despite my opposition to what had been decided!

DROUGHT RELIEF AND THE NJUBI CONVENTION.

Between 1982-1984 Zimbabwe experienced a major drought which affected Matabeleland more than any other area of the country. In addition, due to the 'political problems,' it appears the available 'drought relief' provisions were not reaching certain people in Matabeleland who desperately needed it. At the time

Geoffrey Mkwanasi was in contact with Danie Haarhof, one of the Elders at McChlery. He explained the terrible situation that existed at Matobo and at the business meeting at McChlery Avenue Assembly in Harare they allocated a certain sum of money for 'drought relief.' As this was not far from West Nicholson, on the Bulawayo Beit Bridge Road and a long way from Harare, they sent me the money and asked me to deal with the situation.

I was only too happy to assist and made preparations to go to Matabo. On the first occasion I was accompanied by my wife Mally, our young son Jonathan, and Geoffrey and Eleanor Mkwanazi. In addition, Bernard Maddock, a man in our congregation at Bethshan, accompanied us in his Peugeot van loaded up with supplies. After discussing the needs with Geoffrey, we purchased things like mealie meal, tea, sugar, salt, beans, dried fish and other items. Sadly, the pile of food as the photo will show, was extremely small when divided amongst the families associated with the Assembly. The photo was taken before mealie meal was added which is the staple diet of the people, but even with the mealie meal it was still not a great deal. Despite that, they were all very, very, grateful. We made the trip on at least three occasions and each time the food was divided between an increasing number of people.

Geoffrey and Elenor Mkwanzi, Mally and Jonathan and
the Matabo congregation.
Geoffrey Mkwanazi, Alan and Jonathan, distributing
food.
Bernard Maddox before unloading the food.

It was a real eye opener to visit this drought-stricken
area of the country. I was amazed to discover that at
the height of the drought, not only were there no crops
to be seen, and no grass growing anywhere, but what
really touched my heart, was that there were also no
leaves at all on any of the trees. We made sure that we

73

included maize 'seed,' and some agricultural tools on our final trip to the area. It was important that the community were able to plant 'seed' in the ground when the rain finally returned after the drought.

On one occasion, Geoffrey was not available, and neither was Bernard and my only companion was Eleanor Mkwanasi who was very necessary as my interpreter and guide. On this occasion our very good trailer was loaded up with supplies. But the supplies we purchased in Bulawayo did not include mealie meal, the basic food for the people. We had discovered that we could purchase all that we needed, at a trading store not far from the village. As a result, we went to the store in order to purchase this essential food as soon as we had offloaded the other supplies.

On arrival at the store, we were a little concerned to discover that a platoon of Zimbabwe soldiers was present and enjoying a time of 'rest and refreshment' or R & R. The reason that we were 'a little concerned' was that the 5th Brigade were operating on the other side of the main Bulawayo-Johannesburg Road not far from where we were. Not only that, but when we arrived, the Sergeant in charge was inebriated, and wanted to know what we were doing in the area? After explaining our mission, our conversation went something like this.

The Drunk Sergeant said, **"Buy me a beer when you go into the shop."**

"No," I said, **"I am sorry, I do not drink alcohol and do not encourage others to drink. I can buy you a coke if you like?"**

The Sergeant said, **"No thanks, but you can buy me some cigarettes."**

I replied, **"No, sorry, I do not smoke, and I do not encourage others to smoke."**

As a result of our ongoing conversation, Eleanor became increasingly concerned, but praise God, it eventually came to an end and we were able to enter the store. But, as I had a wad of notes in my pocket, it was rather difficult when I came to pay. I was not keen to reveal the amount of money that I had on my person, and so I slowly withdrew the money one note at a time. Once we had paid for our purchase, we were able to get on our way.

When I look back on this incident I am convinced that we were in a dangerous situation! But I had every confidence that God was with us. What makes me sad, is that I failed to take full advantage of the opportunity that had presented itself outside that store. I am convinced that had I asked my rather drunk Sergeant, he would have given me permission to preach to the whole group. Nevertheless, with no further hold ups, praise God, we were able to accomplish our mission, and distribute the food to the local fellowship.

It was also in 1983 that Geoffrey asked me to preach at the Easter Convention being held at the Njubi Assembly in Bulawayo. We attended as a family, and I considered it a tremendous privilege to minister God's Word at this wonderful Convention. When we arrived for the first meeting, the Assembly was packed to overflowing, however, the people made a way for the Robertson family to enter, and we were ushered right down to the front. The seats that had been prepared for us were then vacated by those who were sitting in them so that we could all sit down. There were a lot of children present but right through the service they sat quietly on one side of the church. If they began to make any noise, they were immediately told to be quiet by one of the elders, who was sitting nearby. They were a real credit to their parents and to the leaders of that fellowship.

Between the services, the people were fed from huge pots of 'sadza' prepared on open fires outside in the Church grounds. 'Sadza' is a thick porridge made from mealie meal and is the staple diet of most Zimbabweans. However, we were given special treatment and taken to a nearby house where a meal was prepared for us all. Geoffrey was away preaching at another 'convention' and so Eleanor Mkwananzi escorted us to the house and we sat at a table while she served us. We asked her to join us but she refused and continued to serve us until we had all eaten. It was only after we had finished that she sat down to eat. Both Geoffrey and Eleanor were lovely people and a real credit to the work of God in Bulawayo and throughout the country.

Years later, when visiting Zimbabwe from the UK in 1998, we paid a surprise visit to the Mkwanazi's in Bulawayo. Geoffrey was in his car and about to go out, but when he saw us, he changed his plans. In fact, he was so pleased to see us that he literally wept on my shoulders. What a gracious couple, it was a pleasure and privilege to work with them.

The other day I discovered that a book has been written about the life of the late Geoffrey Mkwanazi which I hope to acquire in due course. It is entitled,

"DEDICATED SERVICE."

The story of Geoffrey Bixoni Mkwanazi of the Assemblies of God Church.
By Pathisa Nyathi- Amagugu Publishers.

During the weeks before ministering at the Njubi Easter Convention I had been preaching on 'RELATIONSHIPS' at Bethshan. As I would be ministering on a number of occasions that weekend, I decided to deal with a different subject at each of the meetings at Njubi. This resulted in me speaking on 'THE CHRISTIAN AND THE GOVERNMENT' at one of those meetings. In hind sight it was a very delicate subject to have chosen.

But, at that time most of the 'white' community were unaware of the details of what was happening to the Ndebele people in the tribal areas of the country. As time went on more and more details emerged but at the time, I was ignorant about the seriousness of the situation. In the new Zimbabwe Army, there was a unit known as the 5th Brigade which had been trained by the North Koreans and from early 1983 to late 1987 a series of massacres of Ndebele civilians known as Gukurahundi took place in the rural areas of Matabeleland. In addition, thousands of Ndebele were detained without trial and many died. Even some of our Assembly of God Ministers were detained at that time but I will speak more about that later.

Now, when I spoke on 'THE CHRISTIANS AND THE GOVERNMENT' my text was,

"Let every soul be subject to the governing authorities. For there is no authority except from God,

and the authorities that exist are appointed by God."
Romans 13.1

As I was preaching that morning I distinctly remember saying, **"When Ian Smith was the Prime Minister of Rhodesia I submitted to the governing authorities. When Bishop Abel Muzorewa became Prime Minister of Zimbabwe-Rhodesia, I also submitted to the governing authorities and now that Robert Mugabe is Prime Minister of Zimbabwe as a Christian believer I must also submit to the governing authorities."**

I had just finished saying those words when a man on the front row remarked not very quietly, **"We submit, or we die."**

I have never forgotten this very sobering comment on the words that I had spoken!

I have a lovely photo of Geoffrey Mkwanazi and the Elders of the Njubi Assembly standing outside the front door of the building. They were all dedicated men of God and it was a great privilege to have been the guest speaker that weekend.

Geoffrey and Elenor Mkwanazi – Njubi AOG
Bulawayo.
Ministers and Elders at the 1983 Convention.
The Convention Choir.

THE NATIONAL EXECUTIVE OF ZIMBABWE.

It was in October 1977 that the first conference of the newly formed 'Assemblies of God of Rhodesia' took place. The Conference had been organised by a provisional Executive and was held at the Baptist Seminary Camp grounds, seven miles from Gweru. At this conference the first Rhodesian Executive was elected from the 'black' and 'white' delegates who came together from many different parts of the country.

I was not among those elected to that first Rhodesian Executive, which as could be expected, had to deal with some very difficult issues. But I was duly elected at a subsequent Conference in 1981, to the national Executive of Zimbabwe. As a member of the Executive, I was asked to take over Neil Gibb's responsibilities as the National Secretary when he moved to South Africa. I remained in that position until the National Conference in 1986. During that whole time, and long afterwards, Geoffrey Mkwanazi, was the National Chairman. For the record I must add that all our meetings were conducted in a great atmosphere of brotherly love and respect.

Although we were living in the same town, Geoffrey and I would usually travel in our own cars to the Executive meetings. He owned an old red Mercedes, which he drove at a sedate pace, which was possibly one of the reasons that he was often a little late for the meetings. The main reason that we travelled in different cars was due to us having other jobs to do on the way, people to visit etc. Nevertheless, one day Geoffrey's car was out of order, and he asked me to give him a lift to the meeting in Gweru.

I was known to drive a little faster than Geoffrey, and was usually at the meeting before time. As a result, when we arrived at our destination that day, my good friend Geoffrey got out of my car, wiped his brow, and exclaimed, **"Praise God, we made it in one piece!"**

Strange to say I can only remember one occasion

when he asked me for a lift!

During the time that I was Secretary I was invited to visit Hwange, where Simon Mkolo was ministering. After establishing two Assemblies, one at number one colliery and the other one at number two colliery, he challenged his Elders to take the Gospel further afield. It appears that they were unresponsive to his challenge and felt that they already had more than enough to do looking after two congregations. As he was anxious that the Gospel needed to go out to all the land, he came up with a plan which by-passed his Elders.

Simon Mkolo 1989

The plan as I remember it, had three main parts.

1) THE FILM TEAM. A small team of dedicated men would take the 'JESUS' Film to a village for a weekend

outreach. After seeing the film, there were always a number of people who responded and wanted to follow Jesus and these would be duly counselled by the 'Film Team.'

2) THE EVANGELISM TEAM. The following weekend the Evangelism Team would visit the same village to do further evangelism and 'follow up.'

3) THE CHURCH PLANTING TEAM. Following the FILM TEAM, and THE EVANGELISM TEAMS success THE CHURCH PLANTING TEAM would move into the village where they would establish a new Assembly during the following months.

As the Hwange Assembly had very limited resources, all those involved in this work were unpaid volunteers. Many had no other employment, and so were very grateful to receive 'second hand' clothing brought into the country from the UK by Global Literature Lifeline. In addition, they were dependent upon food provided by the villages that they visited. Later on, when one of the team proved that they had the calling of God upon their lives, Simon would arrange for them to attend Bible College. They would usually be sent to the Pentecostal Assemblies of Canada Bible College in Harare. At the end of their training, they would then enter full time ministry.

Although Simon had limited local resources in Hwange, I discovered that he was receiving assistance from a number of different overseas ministries. When I questioned him about some of them, he said, **"They only come for a short time, if they say something that is not correct, I can always set it right after they leave. But I need help to get the word out and get the job done."**

The last time I was in contact with him he advised me that the Hwange Town Council had told him that they could no longer have their annual convention in the town. The reason that they gave was that there were now far too many people attending his conventions. In order to handle the crowds, the only way that they were able to proceed was to have two conventions. One convention, with fewer people attending, was able to be held in Hwange and another one was held in another centre. Praise God for the expansion in the work! He was no longer talking about 'two' large Assemblies in Hwange, he was talking about two separate conventions, with many thousands of people.

My visit was a real blessing to me but I was only able to visit one of his Assemblies during the time that I was there. I had the privilege of staying with his son, and his wife and family. His son had a good job working on the mine and lived in a three bedroomed mine house. The night that I was there it was roasting and I had the fan on in my bedroom all night, something I usually never do. Years later Simon visited us in England on his way to the USA. I am sad to say that I never went out of my way to get to know him better as he was without doubt a great man of God who I highly respect.

THE NATIONAL (ENGLISH LANGUAGE) WORK.

For the remainder of my time in Bulawayo, I continued to minister at Bethshan, in addition to the numerous responsibilities that I had inherited from Neil Gibbs. As more and more of our members were 'taking the gap' and heading for South Africa, Australia, New

Zealand, Canada, the UK and elsewhere, many of our Ministers were doing the same, and one of my responsibilities was to find someone to replace them. It is important to mention that this was a 'one way' stream as during the seven years that I 'led' the 'work' in Zimbabwe, although a lot of our Ministers went South, no South African was willing to come North, except Noel Cromhout who I will mention later in my story.

Another responsibility that I inherited was Secretary of the National Development Fund. The fund, known by some as the 'NEVER DEVELOPING FUND,' had been set up mainly to cover any shortfall that Assemblies had in meeting the 'salaries' of their Ministers. This was confined to the Assemblies working with John Bond, in what I like to call 'The English Language Group.' Each of our Assemblies and all of our Ministers were encouraged to send a 'tithe' of their income to the fund enabling the 'Fund' to respond to any call made upon it during the month. In addition to this, as has been mentioned elsewhere, there was one, and only one Assembly, that contributed over and above a tithe and that was McChlery. It is true to say that without their contributions the fund would never have been able to meet the ongoing needs of the National work.

Yet another job that I inherited, was being the AOG liaison officer with the Marriage Registrar over the appointment of Marriage Officers. In addition to these added responsibilities, just in case you still feel that I only worked on Sundays, I also took over responsibility for arranging ministry on the English Service of the Zimbabwe Broadcasting Corporation.

For many years the RBC and later the ZBC had broadcast a half hour service every Sunday morning, and evening. In addition, there was a very short early morning and lunchtime religious broadcast each week day. This had always been arranged by what are often referred to as the 'established churches' which included the Church of England, Baptists, Methodists, Presbyterians, Roman Catholics, etc. Sometime in the early 1970's it seems that Gary Strong, the Methodist Evangelist, who I have mentioned previously, requested that the Assemblies of God also be included. As a result of his efforts in addition to the 'established churches' we were also invited to participate.

As a result, I was now responsible for arranging for either myself, or one of our other ministers, to record the services at the ZBC when we were required to do so. As you can imagine with each transfer of Neil's former responsibilities to me, his load became lighter, and mine became much heavier.

Despite all this, one of my first responsibilities as leader of the English Language work, was to arrange for a new minister at Redcliff. I had been advised by Neil Gibbs that Allan Rockhill had agreed to replace Stuart MacDonald when he moved to Marondera. Allan had attended ACTS Bible school in Harare after coming to know the Lord under the ministry of Steve Bacon. The first time that I met him was in the presence of Steve at his church in Harare. During our conversation, Steve told us that Len Gibson would be moving to South Africa within a few months. This was news to me as Len was ministering at our Assembly in Hatfield. He then suggested that it would be better if Allan stayed in Harare and took over from Len when he left the country.

I was quite surprised at this suggestion, as I understood from Neil that the decision had already been made. But, despite that, I said that I was not opposed to the idea, and if that was what Allan wanted, we could consider that possibility. However, there was still the pressing need for someone for Redcliff. Having heard what I had to say, Steve said something like the following, **"It is the first time that I have heard someone in leadership in the AOG who was willing to change their mind!"**

Thankfully, after further discussion, Allan agreed to move to Redcliff, as had been previously arranged. I was really grateful to Allan and praised God for helping me so unmistakably in my new role. But, having said that, I think it is a good time to mention what a member of Stuart MacDonald's congregation in Marondera had to say. Apparently, when he heard that I would be leading the work in Zimbabwe under John Bond he exclaimed, **"If AB Robertson is the leader of the Work in Zimbabwe, God help the Assemblies of God."**

When I heard about his comment, instead of being upset, I remember saying something like the following, **"He is absolutely correct, and I totally agree! May God help us! Amen!"**

While still living in Bulawayo we had a Ministers' and Elders' Meeting at McChlery with Lawrence Wilson as our guest speaker. Some years before, he and his wife Margaret, were among the many who had gone out into the Ministry from McChlery Avenue and moved to South Africa. We had a great time of fellowship, and the ministry that we received from Lawrence was appreciated by all, but as we were going next door for lunch, Lawrence turned to me and said, **"AB, don't try so hard!"**

It seems that the burden of my new responsibilities, must have been visible to my friend, otherwise he would never have made such a remark!

The building next door had been purchased by the Assembly, and Marion Van Gent was running a very successful Nursery School on the premises! It was the ideal place for us to have lunch although I think that many of the chairs were a little small.

It was also at the beginning of 1983 that a new minister was required for Kwe Kwe. The previous minister, Gary Smith, had done an incredible work in the town, with something like 200 people being won to Christ during the short period that he was there. Sadly, the Assembly did not grow much during this time as during the same period around 200 people left for South Africa. Following his success in Kwe Kwe, he was moved by John Bond to Chinhoyi and then down to South Africa.

In any case, John Potter set up a meeting for me with John Baker, who like Allan Rockhill had just completed his training at Acts Bible College in Harare. He and some others were planning to go to the Seychelles with the view to share the Gospel on those islands, but the project had failed to materialise and John Baker was wondering what he should do when John Potter suggested that he talk to me.

The story that John Baker told me of how he came to Christ was really quite amazing. He had been in the Royal Navy and part of the 'Beira Patrol' stopping oil in particular from being imported into

Rhodesia, through the port of Beira. He then left the Royal Navy, and settled in Rhodesia, and became part of the Rhodesian 'Navy' patrolling the waters of Lake Kariba. At that time, he was a hard drinking man who had no time for God, but God, was about to move in his life.

As I remember the story, an American Missionary had established a congregation in Kariba and had invited John to church. Sadly, John had very little time for Americans, or church, and made it clear that he was not interested. It was then that the missionary asked his congregation to pray for 5 specific people to get saved in the town. He told them that they were to pray for the people that they considered the most unlikely people to respond. When they had completed their lists, it was discovered that John was at the top of all of their lists as the most unlikely man to respond to the Gospel in Kariba.

Anyhow, John eventually attended church and miraculously came to know Jesus as his Lord and Saviour. He then resigned from his work patrolling Lake Kariba and enrolled in Acts Bible College in Harare determined to serve the Lord. Having met up with John and Shelia, and with a good report from John Potter, I was happy to offer them the opportunity of taking on the Pastorate of our Assembly in Kwe Kwe. But before agreeing to take on the job, John went to see Richmond Chiundiza, one of the men who had ministered to him at Bible College. He had many questions on his heart and needed some advice. After sharing his concerns with this dear brother, Richmond apparently said something like the following, **"The**

Assembly of God need a minister, and you need a job. What's the problem! You do not need any guidance, God has opened a door for you, all you need to do is go through the door."

As a result, John agreed to move to Kwe Kwe, and I introduced John and Sheila to the congregation, laid hands on them and prayed that God would bless and use them in their ministry. Praise God, they were able to successfully lead the Assembly until 1986 when they moved to Harare.

It was not long before I discovered that what Steve Bacon had told me was correct, as Len Gibson was moving to South Africa. In fact, before the year was out, we needed a new Minister for Hatfield.

Under Len's leadership, the Assembly had amalgamated with another Pentecostal Fellowship in the area. As a result, they had one Elder, and two good deacons capable of caring for the work when Len and his wife left for South Africa. When I discovered what was happening, I contacted the leaders of the Assembly and told them that just as soon as I had someone available, I would be in touch.

There was nothing that I could do, as I had no one available. Nevertheless, sometime later I had a call from Steve Bacon who said that Paul Croft could be the man that we needed for Hatfield. Paul had come to Christ at Mabelreign Chapel under Don Normond's ministry. After training for the ministry at 'Christ for the Nations Bible College in Dallas Texas' he returned to the country and pastored a Church in Macheke for some time. However, after doing a good work among the farmers in the area, he spent a short time working with Steve Bacon at Strathhaven but was now looking for a new position.

Having heard what Steve had to say, I travelled up to Harare and, accompanied by Roland Pletts, I met with Steve and Paul at the Jameson Hotel in Harare. I was immediately taken with Paul whom I could see was a man of God. After some discussion it was agreed that he should go to Hatfield. We agreed on a date and I phoned the leaders in Hatfield with the good news.

But, much to my surprise, I was advised that they were in the process of bringing a man up from South Africa to fill the post in Hatfield. I said that it was all news to me as I had been looking for someone to fill the post ever since Len Gibson had left. I then asked who they were in contact with and why I had not been advised? The man that I was talking to then told me that Hatfield was not an Assembly of God fellowship as it was an amalgamation of more than two congregations. As I had previously been the Pastor of the Hatfield Assembly of God, at the time when we put the sign up to advertise who we were, I replied, "**That's news to me!**"

After some discussion it was arranged that we call a special church meeting to discuss the issue. Once I put the phone down, I realised that I had better let Paul Croft know about these new developments.

"**Good evening, Paul,**" I said, "**We have a problem. If you go to Hatfield, you may only be going to an Assembly with a half a dozen people. It sounds as if a lot of the people are planning to leave and start a new fellowship.**"

Paul replied, "**No problem, AB, whether there are few or many I believe it is of God that I go to Hatfield and so I am still happy to go.**"

After some discussion, it was agreed that Paul

would accompany me to the meeting in Hatfield that Saturday. But, having heard what Paul had to say, after telling him that he may well only have a half a dozen people in the congregation, I could have cried. His words were such an encouragement to me. I put the phone down and believed that God would see us through.

On the Saturday afternoon, Paul Croft accompanied me to a meeting at Hatfield where the whole congregation came together. We spent some time discussing the situation but it became increasingly clear that there was going to be a split in the Assembly.

The leading spokesman, one of the Deacons, announced that they would be leaving the Assembly and starting a new fellowship. He also announced where they would be meeting and what time the service would be the following morning. After he had finished, I said, **"I will be preaching here tomorrow, and next Sunday your new Minister, Paul Croft, will be taking the services."**

However, as most of the people who were leaving the Assembly had made contributions to the funds held in our account, I went on to say, **"As soon as you have opened a Bank Account in the name of your new fellowship, please let me know the details. You will need to purchase song books, chairs and many other things and I would like to help. When you let me know, I will send you a cheque of Z$1000.00 to help you get established."**

In a spirit of goodwill, I was prepared to assist them in their endeavours. I am not too sure what John Bond would have thought of my generosity, however, if we were to have a 'split' then I did not want any hard feelings, we were after all 'brethren!'

It was at that moment that Barry White asked if we had all finished. He was a recognised Elder in the Assembly, and had been the chairman of the meeting that afternoon. When we said that we had finished, he told us that he had an announcement to make and said, **"After considering prayerfully what I should do I have come to the conclusion that I should remain here at the Hatfield Assembly. My wife and I will not be leaving."**

Naturally, I was thrilled with such a surprising conclusion to the matters of the day and within less than two months nearly all of the people who had left were back in fellowship under Paul Croft's able leadership. In addition, the Lord was clearly watching over me as no one ever asked me to provide the Z$1000.00 that I had promised. Praise God, we serve a wonderful Saviour!

In 1981, Andy Murlis, who had been ministering at Bulawayo North, was asked by John Bond to move to Marondera and Idris Davies took his place. Sadly, while they were at Bulawayo North, Idris's dear wife Iris went to be with the Lord. Then in September 1983, as the representative of John Bond, I asked Idris if he would move to Chinhoyi to take over the Assembly there. Sadly, it was then that I lost my assistant, as Simon Rhodes moved over to Bulawayo North.

I remember getting a lot of criticism from various quarters as Idris was now an old man, and he had recently buried his dear wife, however, none of the criticism came from Idris himself. He was always gracious, and responded to this latest call upon his life and moved to Chinoyi where he remained until his death in April 1986.

By this time, I was ministering at McChlery Avenue Assembly in Harare and was asked by the family to conduct the funeral service. Idris was a lovely man of God who had laboured for many years as an Elder, and after his retirement as a valued member of our team in Zimbabwe. He had willingly set aside his own preferences and moved to Chinoyi and laboured there until God called him home. I remember going to visit him in hospital shortly before he died and despite his lifelong commitment to the Lord I said, **"Dear brother, it seems strange to have to do this but I feel that I must. Are you ready to go home? Are you ready to meet the Lord?"**

He assured me that he was, and I left soon afterwards and did not see him again. Regrettably, I fear that I did not do him justice at his funeral in April 1986. Because of this, I very belatedly honour my brother and thank him for all that he did, and although he entered into his reward many years ago, I honour him as a valuable member of the Assemblies of God in Rhodesia/Zimbabwe who was sadly missed.

At the end of 1983, I was asked by John Bond to move back to Harare and take over the leadership of McChlery Avenue Assembly. It was agreed that Gary Smith, who was not happy in South Africa, should return to Zimbabwe, and replace me at Bethshan. I was very happy with my replacement as Gary had done an exceptional work in Kwe Kwe and I knew that he would do well at Bethshan, his home Assembly. However, there was a problem, as Gary was anxious to move and get settled before the beginning of the school year. Sadly, for a number of reasons we were unable to move immediately, mainly because the Manse was occupied in Harare. A well known and loved Portuguese family were living in the property until they were able to leave the country. Nevertheless, because Gary was anxious to move, possibly because of pressures in South Africa, we moved out of the house to enable him and his family to move in.

As we had nowhere to go, we initially stayed in a mobile home owned by one of the members of the congregation. It was difficult, and I ought not to have agreed to move, as my wife, Mally, was pregnant with our fourth child at the time. However, we survived, and as soon as we could, we moved up to Harare.

It had been an incredible few years in Bulawayo and although we had a few rough patches we made a lot of good friends and left with some wonderful memories. How could one forget, 'THE MUSIC MACHINE,' 'THE CANTATA,' and 'THE CITY WIDE CRUSADE' and so much more. In addition, how could we ever forget all the wonderful people that we had worked with in Bulawayo. Hallelujah, God is so good!

B) McCHLERY AVENUE ASSEMBLY HARARE. 1984 to July 1986

As I have already mentioned, I was asked by John Bond to take over the leadership of McChlery Avenue Assembly in Harare at the end of 1983. I was more than happy to do so as the Lord had shown me very clearly, that this would happen. We were still unpacking in Chipinge in 1978, when I knew that at some point, we would move back to my home Assembly. It was only now, some five years later, that it was coming to pass.

Sadly, the reason John Bond asked me to move to Harare was that a serious disagreement had arisen within the oversight of the Assembly. The problem, as I understood it, was mainly centred around the Saturday night "Breaking of Bread."

THE SATURDAY NIGHT BREAKING OF BREAD.

My good friend Roland Pletts, who was the senior Minister at the time, felt that the traditional Saturday night Breaking of Bread had outlasted its usefulness. In the past it had been the highlight of the week. Christians from all over town had come to enjoy the powerful meetings which took place every Saturday night. However, those days had gone and things had changed dramatically.

One of the reasons that the Saturday night Breaking of Bread was such a powerful meeting, was that we always encouraged the 'Open Ministry.' This meant that if you had a 'word' from the Lord you were encouraged to get up and share it. There were times when so many wanted to speak, that you had to be on your feet very quickly or else someone would beat you to it. They were great times, and it was the place where many prospective 'ministers' of the Gospel, including myself, first learned to preach.

The 'open ministry' was 'open' to young and old. One Saturday night a young schoolboy got up to speak and in order to illustrate the agelessness of Almighty God, he said, **"God is not old, like brother Mullen!"**

Brother Mullen, who was present that evening, was a great man of God, and a great deal older than the speaker. The congregation that evening was highly amused at how this young man chose to illustrate the agelessness of God. To his credit, as he and his lovely wife Mary were known for their sense of humour, Jim Mullen, also appreciated the illustration.

Before continuing to speak about the Saturday night Breaking of Bread at McChlery, I would like to return to the days when I was a deacon in that same fellowship. I was on 'door duty' one Sunday evening and the Gospel meeting had already started when I saw two men walking down the path to the Assembly from the car park. The one man was dressed in a suit and tie and the other was dressed as a 'hippie.' He had long hair, was dressed in jeans and an open-necked shirt and, if I remember correctly, his shoes were made out of old motor car tyres. As I looked at these men as they approached me this is what crossed my mind, **"The well-dressed man is a Christian who usually attends another church. Maybe they do not have a Sunday evening Gospel service and as a result he has brought this 'hippie' to our service this evening."**

I welcomed them both but was very surprised to find myself counselling Eddie, the well-dressed man, after the meeting. As I sat in front of him, I was even more surprised when he told me, **"I want to make a decision this evening to serve the Lord. I have seen such a change in my brother-in-law (the hippie) since he committed his life to Christ in Johannesburg that I want to follow Jesus as well."**

The 'hippie' and his entire family were soon in fellowship with us and they were a blessing to us all. His youngest sister was so 'radical' when she got saved that, if I am correct, she was asked to leave her junior school as she was always speaking about Jesus. Martin (the hippie) was often encouraged by members of the fellowship to get a haircut but I resisted speaking to him about his appearance. But when I was visiting him one day, he said, **"AB, what do you think about my long hair?"**

We had many long discussions, but the reason I have included this story at this time was as a result of recent communication that we have had together. I include a copy of an email that I received from Brazil on the 11th June, 2021, where Martin Cooper is now a Minister of the Gospel.

"Great to hear from you, AB. Yes, life "in Christ" is never boring, and we are privileged to be part of God's plan all the time. McChlery Ave. was a major change for me, even though I was still very young and understanding little (somewhat rebellious also) looking back the believers showed tolerance and extended grace toward me. Now I see, then I didn't, I remember well after attending meetings for a month or so, someone in the prayer group said to me that they had all been praying for my salvation - believing that Eddie was saved and that's what counts. One thing that I have noted since 1971-2 and living in UK, Brazil, Australia, Zimbabwe, back to Australia, and back to Brazil where I am today is that in all the many churches I have attended, I have never seen such a complete body ministry by demonstrations of spiritual gifts, tongues, interpretation, words of knowledge, prophesy, etc. as would flow orderly at the Saturday night communion meetings. Yes, I have seen all these things and more here and there but

never such a wholesome body building meeting week after week, yes, the Lord was good to us all and we have all received of His fullness and grace for grace.

I was called to the ministry in 1995 in Australia, and have been up the mountains and down the valleys ever since teaching and sharing the good news, so you see you planted well, the Lord watered and I grew. ------------.

All for now, AB
Joyfully walking with Jesus,
Martin Cooper

As you can see from what Martin Cooper has said, the Saturday night Breaking of Bread at McChlery is even remembered today by someone in Brazil. Having read what he has said, I am positive that the Saturday night meeting at McChlery is also remembered today by many of those who had the privilege of attending those powerful meetings.

But things had changed, the numbers had dropped, and the meeting was a shadow of what it had been in the past. The two Ministers, Roland and John Potter, who had recently returned from Bible College at Christ for the Nations in the USA, were of the opinion that the meeting should be closed down. They believed that the Breaking of Bread should be held on a Sunday morning but not necessarily every Sunday. But the Elders were completely opposed to this as they had enjoyed a regular Breaking of Bread every Saturday night for many years. Although the numbers attending the meeting had certainly dropped, they believed that it was not a good enough reason to discontinue the meeting.

It is important to point out that McChlery had absorbed the members of 'THE GRANGE' Assembly when it closed due to the changing situation in the country. 'THE GRANGE' which had originally been started by Neil Gibbs had always had a Sunday Morning Breaking of Bread and most of the former members saw no reason to attend a Saturday Night meeting at McChlery.

Just in case my readers are puzzled as to why we 'broke bread' on a Saturday night and why it was considered so important to the Elders of the Assembly, let us consider a few facts. First of all, we need to remember that the BREAKING OF BREAD or the Communion Service is known in Scripture as the LORD'S SUPPER, and not the LORD'S BREAKFAST. The apostle Paul had this to say to the Christians at Corinth,

"Therefore, when you come together in one place, it is not to eat the Lord's Supper. ------------."
1 Corinthians 11.20

Then a few verses further on, in the portion that we usually read at the Breaking of Bread, he said: -

"In the same manner He also took the cup after supper, saying, ----." 1 Corinthians 11.25

So, it is clear that it was originally an evening meeting. We need to remember that when the Lord Jesus instituted the BREAKING OF BREAD, He was celebrating the PASSOVER. This was a feast day of the Lord which he shared with His disciples just before He was arrested and then later Crucified. This Passover meal was so important to the Lord Jesus that He is recorded as having said,

"-----. With fervent desire I have desired to eat this Passover with you before I suffer, for I say to you, I will no longer eat of it until it is fulfilled in the kingdom of God." Luke 22.15-16

Once again, we need to remember that the PASSOVER celebrates the deliverance of the people of Israel from slavery in Egypt. The night when they were finally delivered every family was eating the 'PASSOVER' lamb behind closed doors, with the blood of the lamb painted on the door posts and lintel of the door. That night, when God sent the angel of death throughout the land of Egypt, if he did not see the 'blood' applied to the door-posts and the lintel of a house the first born male in that house died. This all happened at night and that is why we celebrated the Lord's Supper on a Saturday night! But why SATURDAY you may ask?

"Now on the first day of the week, when the disciples came together to break bread, Paul, ready to depart the next day, spoke to them and continued his message until midnight."
Acts 20.7

We need to remember that for the Jews the 7th and last day of the week was the Sabbath which is of course Saturday and not Sunday as some mistakenly think. However, for the Jews the 'Sabbath day' began in the evening, of what we call Friday and so Saturday evening was the beginning of the FIRST DAY OF THE WEEK which we call Sunday.

The Breaking of Bread that Paul attended must have started at night as he preached until midnight. By then at least one person felt it was time for Paul to stop as he fell asleep, and fell out of a window. He fell from the third story of the building and was taken up dead, however after Paul 'fell on him and embraced him' he was able to say that he was alive and they were not to worry. After that Paul continued to speak until daylight when he had to leave. Paul definitely had the gift of 'continuation.' Please note, that the meeting was held on Saturday night!

Now, before I arrived at McChlery Avenue, a challenging situation had developed. The Saturday night meeting was now being conducted by the Elders on their own, the Sunday morning meeting was usually led by Roland, and John had the responsibility for the Sunday evening Gospel meetings. In order to bring the Assembly together again I made it quite clear to all the oversight that although I understood Roland and John's point of view, we would not close the Saturday night Breaking of Bread unless all the oversight were in agreement. Having made that clear I made a point of being at all the meetings.

But, praise God, there was a solution on the way and sometime after I arrived at McChlery things took a dramatic turn when one day I was approached by André Silcox, who said, **AB, I have been giving it a lot of thought and prayer and think that we ought to close the Saturday night Breaking of Bread."**

"Are you sure Andre?" I asked, **"Would the other Elders support you in this?"**

"Yes, I think it is the most sensible thing to do and we all agree," he replied.

"Well as long as you are sure, I think we

101

should announce it this Saturday night. We will make next Saturday the last meeting and from then on we will break bread on Sunday mornings," I said.

Having received the backing of all the Elders, that Saturday night I made an announcement. **"As from next week we will no longer be meeting on a Saturday night to Break Bread. In future we will Break Bread on a Sunday morning."**

There is no doubt that those who had been faithful members of McChlery for many years were disappointed, however, most were happy to go along with the new arrangements. Having made this decision, there was one interesting development that caught me completely by surprise. It was a couple of weeks after our last Saturday night Breaking of Bread that I visited the Christian bookshop in Harare, which was always well-stocked. As I was browsing through the books I was accosted by the senior minister of a local Church.

The man concerned was Alistair Geddes, the Minister of "Faith Fellowship," a fairly new, but very successful congregation in Harare that was reaching a very multiracial group of people. Unbeknown to me, Alistair had attended our Saturday night Breaking of Bread service on numerous occasions in the past. When he saw me, he told me in no uncertain terms how disappointed he was that we had closed the meeting down and that no one had let him know. I was completely taken by surprise, and also rather annoyed as he was not a member of our congregation!

In hind sight, we should have given a few weeks' notice before closing down a meeting that had been a regular for so many years. However, due to the difficulties that we had experienced at McChlery, once the decision had been taken, I felt that we should act on it without delay. My meeting with Alistair revealed to me how much the Saturday Night Breaking of Bread had become part of the church scene in Harare and how much it was going to be missed. But it also made clear to me that you cannot please all of the people all of the time. Praise God, Alistair has continued to labour faithfully for the Lord and has always been a blessing to the body of Christ and he was forgiven many years ago for getting cross with me!

BUILDINGS AND BEGGARS.

I am not sure when this was done but I will tell the story here. The minor hall was separated from the main building by a narrow passage that was open to the elements. When it rained it was a problem and so we agreed to put a roof on the narrow passage. We also installed a security gate at both ends which gave us a small but very usable space in between the two buildings that could be used during all kinds of weather.

But the problem was the floor! I wanted to put down some nice tiles to make the place look presentable, however, the Elders did not want to spend too much money. Their heart was to give as much money away as possible and not to spend too much on ourselves. I was not opposed to their generosity but, a tiled floor would have made such a difference. Sadly, that is not what I got but, praise God, no one ever called it ABs Folly in Harare as far as I know!

When working in my office at the Assembly, one of the things that I did not like were the number of beggars who came to the door. As mentioned, we now had a security gate which was a blessing and so the office area was not open to the street. But almost every day we had visitors. In Kwe Kwe and Mutare the 'visitors' had been mainly down and out 'white' men, but in Harare they were all 'black' men.

They all had a story to tell, and some, but not all, were obviously real. I was a busy man and really did not have time to listen to story after story. In addition, as the Assembly did not pay me an allowance for my generosity, whatever I parted with was money out of my own pocket.

As mentioned previously, when I was in Bulawayo I had preached on the subject,

"If anyone will not work, neither shall he eat." 2 Thessalonians 3.10

In the Old Testament, in God's agricultural economy, the farmer was required to leave the 'gleanings' of the harvest in the field for the poor to come and reap. They would have to 'work' for their 'free' food and not just receive it on a plate. I believe that generally people are not keen to receive 'charity,' they would much prefer to 'earn' their living. As a result, when these needy men came to the 'gate' I would usually give them a job of work to do. When they had done what I asked them to do I would reward them. Most of them were very happy to be given some small job to do and receive some cash in return. However, one day I gave a man a harder job than usual, and when I went out to check on him, he had gone. Most likely, he left to see if he could find someone else to take pity on him.

It was really frustrating, as I knew that most of them were needy people! But I did not have the time, money, or resources to do anything worthwhile for them. When I returned home, I would sometimes share my frustrations with the family. I would tell them about these men who were constantly coming around to the church. One day as I was dropping the boys off at school Mark turned to me and said, **"Remember what you said, Dad! You said, that you were not going to give anything away to beggars today."**

It was true, I was determined, I had had enough! I was tired of the beggars that continually came to the Assembly every day. But they were my famous last words, as we had five 'visitors' that morning all asking for help and guess what, they all received something.

CHANGES AT McCHLERY.

Only a few months after I arrived in Harare, in April 1984, Allan Rockhill moved to South Africa and John Potter was asked by John Bond to move to Redcliff. Sadly, as a result of all that had taken place, it was not long before Roland Pletts also left McChlery. He later resigned from the movement in order to continue his ministry independently. He was an anointed preacher, and around that time, he took a series of meetings in Harare, speaking on 'THE END TIMES.' The interest in the subject was so great that the large Dutch Reformed Church Hall in the Centre of Harare was filled to capacity. The departure of Roland from the movement was without doubt a real loss.

Recently, I have reread a book that Roland wrote about his ministry in Zimbabwe. It is called **'THE**

LORD REIGNS' and is really worth reading. He writes with passion about the tragedy of what has taken place in our homeland. As he left some years after I left the country, it deals with a lot that happened after we moved to the UK.

Having lost the ministry of both Roland Pletts and John Potter, it was a blessing to have Steve and Linda Bowen join us at McChlery. They had both been teachers before entering the ministry and proved to be a blessing and among other things they organised a very successful Youth Camp at Lake McIlwaine while they were with us.

Due to the ongoing changes taking place in the country, our congregation was changing. As an example, during one year at McChlery, I counted as many as 100 men, women, and children who had left our fellowship, 'taken the gap,' and left the country. Yet despite this ongoing loss, praise God, we were also seeing some new people come into fellowship.

Not all of the new people were 'white' as we were now getting people from all the different racial groups in the community. One of the 'black' families that joined us proved to be a real asset, and the man was very soon made a deacon. They were a lovely family with a heart for the work of God but sadly, I have not remembered their names. When we were considering purchasing a vehicle to pick up children for the Sunday School, we were very grateful when he came forward and donated a VW Kombi.

At about this time, we were joined by a British school teacher who was in the country to assist in the educational effort of the government. He was quite an evangelist, and soon, a number of students that he had led to the Lord began to attend our services. Although all the students could speak English, they had relatives in the area who started attending the services who were not fluent in the language. As a result, I became concerned that they were not getting much out of the service and approached our 'black' deacon and our British school teacher with an alternative plan. I suggested that we have a Sunday afternoon Shona language service in order to cater for the people who were unable to speak English. I made it clear that the 'deacon' would run the meeting under my authority, but the 'teacher' would do most of the preaching which would be interpreted into Shona.

Sadly, when I told the British school teacher what I proposed, he immediately accused me of being a racist. He said that I was planning to have a separate meeting for the 'blacks' in the afternoon to exclude them from the morning meeting. This was not the purpose at all. No one was being excluded from the morning meeting, all I was trying to do was provide a meeting where our new, non-English speaking congregation would be able to understand the service and come to know Jesus as Lord and Saviour.

Despite this shaky start, the meeting was a success and very soon we had a good number of people attending. Sadly, our deacon was criticised by some of those attending the afternoon meeting for still wanting to attend the English service in the morning. They told him that he ought to remain in the Shona service as he was a black man! It was a difficult time in Zimbabwe!

In addition to the people already mentioned, we were blessed to have two Lecturers from the University of Zimbabwe attend our meetings. They were a lovely Christian couple from Ghana who had taken up positions at our local University. When I went to visit them at the University, I remember asking them how they were paid as expatriates working in Zimbabwe? They told me that only part of their salary was paid to them in Zimbabwe and the rest was paid into a Bank in London. They were not happy to have their wages paid into the Bank in Ghana as they were not sure that they would ever receive the money. What a sad situation for these people from Ghana. They could not trust the authorities in their home country to look after their money!

RESTHAVEN.

As the church Manse was still unavailable when we moved, after considering a number of options, we managed to find temporary accommodation at Resthaven with the help of John Dunn. This was a Christian retreat and conference centre about 15 miles north of Harare. We enjoyed our short stay in that beautiful, peaceful valley, despite it being some distance from town. While living there, two things happened that I would like to mention.

The first one involved our eldest son, Mark, who had developed a problem while we were living in Chipinge. Our doctor had been unable to diagnose what the problem was and he had suffered a great deal of pain on a number of occasions during the four years since that time. One of those occasions was when we were on holiday in South Africa, and another was while we were filming the Music Machine at the ZBC in

Bulawayo.

One day whilst living at Resthaven, I arrived home only to discover that Mally had taken Mark to the A&E at the hospital and, praise God, the problem had at last been diagnosed. It was discovered that he had kidney stones and after passing a number of stones he was finally free from the pain. It had been a real mystery, no one expected a young boy, Mark's age, to have such a problem but, praise God, it was over!

The next incident involved our youngest son, Jonathan. He had a bicycle, which still had stabilisers fitted, but no brakes. Having read my 'Early Life' you may wonder why this was a problem, as I had ridden a bike for years with no brakes! However, this was not ME, this was my little son! I decided to visit the workshop at Resthaven to see if there was someone on hand who could fix the brakes for us. You need to understand that all our possessions were still packed away and we were living out of suitcases. I did not have any tools to do the job and in any case as has already been mentioned I was not a handy man!

I was accompanied by Mark and Matthew on our way to the workshop, and Jonathan came on his bike. The trip was uphill on a very rough road and sadly, our visit proved to be unsuccessful. As we turned around to return to our temporary home down the hill, we were taken by surprise when Jonathan started to move rapidly down the hill on his bike in front of us. As I chased after him, he left the road, and began to travel faster and faster down the very steep grass slope. I was horrified to see that he was heading straight for a standing water pipe which was directly in his path! There was nothing that I could do to stop him.

Suddenly, not more than a foot or two from the pipe, he came off his bike, which most likely saved him from serious harm.

If you remember, whilst we were in India, I mentioned that we could well have met up with an angel on one occasion? On that day, when we were feeling really discouraged, a man came out of nowhere, who was such an encouragement to us. As I am typing this story it seems to me that it may well have been an angel who gave Jonathan a push that day, saving him from serious harm. Whatever it was, we were so very grateful, and praised God for His deliverance!

Following this incident, I was concerned that Jonathan might be too nervous to ride his bike. But praise God, despite his adventure, our little boy had no problems. God is so good!

HILLSIDE.

Finally, the house was available and we were able to move into the Manse at 15 Newmarch Avenue in Hillside. It was a lovely family home which had previously belonged to members of the Assembly who had since emigrated. There was a swimming pool in the back garden which proved to be a blessing to all the family. Sadly, there was a drought when we were living there, and because of water rationing, we were not able to keep it full. Another problem was that it had a leak which was never repaired while we were there. As a result, I made sure that when it rained, all the rainwater from the roof was channeled into the pool.

It was in this pool that our sons first began to swim. One day Mark and Matthew had a race to see who could swim across the pool first. Although it was only 'doggie paddle,' our second born son, Matthew, won the race. Our sons made friends with many of the local 'black' children and almost every afternoon a number of them could be found in our swimming pool. But, one day, our servant Cosmos, a big man, decided enough was enough, and he chased them all away. He was tired of all the noise that they were making, as it was distracting him from his work.

Our eldest son was enrolled at the nearby Eastridge Junior School. Sadly, things did not work out well for him as his class teacher, a lady of mixed race, had very little control over the mainly 'black' pupils. He would come home from school and inform us that he was not learning anything as the students were so noisy that he could not hear. We learned many years later, that amongst other things, another teacher used to pick on him constantly in class. It was clear that we would have to move as soon as possible so that Mark could attend a different school. Our second son, Matthew, had much more success at John McChlery School. This was a well-run infant school, just across the road from where we lived, where Mrs. Hackitt was the Headmistress.

LUKE ROBERTSON.

As already mentioned, my wife, Mally, was pregnant with our fourth child when we left Bulawayo. This was despite being warned not to have any more children when Jonathan was born. Due to our different blood types Jonathan had to have all his blood drained away and a new lot of blood inserted in his body soon after he was born. Praise God, he was a healthy child, but another child was on the way.

Everything went fine until almost the time for the birth of our baby boy. Sadly, he was still born which was a real tragedy for both of us, but I was not the mother! My wife, Mally, had been through her most difficult pregnancy, and carried Luke, as we named him, for the full term, and then at the very last moment she lost the child. It was a very difficult time for her!

We were very grateful for the support that we received from all the oversight at McChlery as well as from the congregation. Quite a few attended baby Luke's burial service. Their prayers, and encouragement were a great blessing to both of us and helped us to move on Despite our loss.

HIGHLANDS.

As a result of Mark's experiences at school, towards the end of 1984, we began to look for another house. We needed to find a house in Highlands for the boys to be able to attend Highlands Junior School as we were not in the correct zone living in Hillside. When they knew that we were looking for a house in Highlands, a couple who were members of the Assembly offered us their house as they were moving back to Scotland.

The house was ideal and the price was right and so a deal was struck and we were on our way. The address of our new home was 6, Kensington Road Highlands. It was within walking distance of the school but on the other side of the very busy Enterprise Road. At the beginning of 1985, our sons, Mark and Matthew, were both able to start at their new school. It was amazing the difference it made to Mark! He had hardly learned anything at his previous school but now his class teacher took a real interest in him and he caught up on all that he had missed. By the end of the year, from being near the bottom of his class, he had moved up to second place.

One day I arrived to pick up the boys, and discovered that Mark was very upset. He had purchased an ice cream from one of the vendors, parked at the school gate, and paid for it with a one dollar note. Although he had already finished eating his ice cream, he was still waiting for his change, which up until then had not been forthcoming. It is possible that the vendor did not have any change when Mark purchased his ice cream, as he immediately gave him his change when I went up to him with my son!

Our son, Matthew, thrived in his new school, particularly when it came to sports. During the annual sports day in 1988, he came 5th in the cross country, and 3rd in the high jump, proving that he did not take after his dad! He also started playing tennis and was very soon chosen for the school team. When we returned to Bulawayo at the end of 1988, his sports teacher made a point of telling us how disappointed she was to see him leave, as she had invested so much time in training him!

We really appreciated the understanding that the elders at McChlery showed us by assisting us in our move to Highlands. It was decided to sell the Hillside property to pay for the one in Highlands as it seemed the best way to handle the situation at the time. However, in hind sight I have always felt that it was the wrong move. I was not the 'business man' but a number of my leaders were, and not long afterwards we were paying rent for a house for one of my assistants when we should have 'owned' a house for them to live in. It was a difficult time but the Assembly would have easily been able to raise the deposit, pay a mortgage, and if necessary, they could have sold the house later as not long after this the price of houses went sky high.

Our youngest son, Jonathan, began his schooling at the Nursery School run by Marion van Gent at McChlery. It was a really good start for him, as the school was excellent, and the love of Christ was evident to all.

Continuing with our 'family' affairs, Mally found temporary employment working at a Nursing Home when we were living in Harare. One of the nurses working there was the wife of a Canadian missionary by the name of Glen Kauffeldt. He was the senior Missionary in Zimbabwe working with the Pentecostal Assemblies of Canada and we became good friends.

The 'nursing home cat' gave birth to a number of offspring and one day Mally arrived home with one of the kittens. This was the thin edge of the wedge, and before we left Harare, we had three dogs and a cat and could well have moved back to Bulawayo with a large number of Bantam chickens as well but for the following incident.

Yes, not only did we have three dogs and a cat whilst living at 6 Kensington Road in Highlands but we also ended up with some chickens. When our son, Mark, showed interest in her lovely Bantam chickens, our neighbour, Mrs. Winter (Billy Winter's mother) was kind enough to give him two hens and a cockerel. Billy Winter had preached the message at the South African General Conference in 1969 which had made such an impact upon me. It was not long before the three Bantam chickens had multiplied and we had a dozen or more. As a result, Mark seriously considered going into the chicken business, -------- but then disaster struck!

Before continuing with the bantams, I must backtrack a little. After we acquired our first little kitten, we later acquired another one. Sadly, one day I discovered the first cat dead at the bottom of our garden. We were convinced that it had been poisoned as one of our dogs also begun to act rather strangely. We had a large garden but when the postman came to the gate the dogs would go wild and cause no end of a fuss running all the way around the inside of the property barking like mad. In addition, one of the delivery men was bitten on one occasion. We had not 'trained' them to behave like that but it is possible that someone had taken exception and tried to poison the dogs.

But on the other hand, it may well have had something to do with the break-in we had one night. The dogs woke me up, as they were going mad barking and rushing around the garden. The thief managed to break into the house using the key that we had left in the lock inside the house. Praise God, he only got away with a portable radio/tape recorder which we had recently purchased whilst in South Africa. It could have been worse had the dogs not barked. There was an expensive projector sitting in the same room belonging to the Assembly, but praise God, it was still there in the morning. The main house (not counting the outside bedroom) had a total of four separate outside doors. The thief had come into the house by one door, I had gone out of the house to investigate by another door, while he vacated the house by yet another door. He was in and out before the dogs knew where he was.

In any case, remaining with the dogs, I brought Len Marrillier back to the house one day for lunch. As we drove through the gates the dogs came running up and Len exclaimed, **"AB, are your dogs South African?"**

I knew exactly what he was saying as Len was a South African of mixed race, and he wondered whether our dogs would take exception to him because he was not 'white' and so I replied, **"Yes, however we never trained them that way. In any case they will be fine as soon as they know that you are one of our friends."**

Getting back to the 'chickens,' one Sunday morning we arrived back home from the meeting to find the garden strewn with feathers and when we looked closely, we discovered that all the Bantams were dead. Our usually placid dog had killed the lot! We were stunned, and understandably our son, Mark, was very upset as he loved his Bantams.

This incident must have taken place shortly before we left for Bulawayo as Mark never had the opportunity to start his 'chicken business' again. On arrival in Bulawayo our dog would often drink from the swimming pool and surprisingly he was soon restored to full health. Not as a result of drinking the swimming pool water, but as a result of being taken away from whatever was poisoning his system.

We had a large garden and one day I asked Cosmos our very willing servant to assist in building a

BMX race track around the back garden. When I say 'assist' I really mean that he built the BMX track! From then on, our boys and their friends had a great deal of fun racing around the garden on their own private BMX track. It was very noisy when this was going on and possibly quite dangerous as well. There was not a 'health and safety expert' in sight! Praise God, we never had any serious problems and they all had great fun!

It was whilst we were living in Harare that John Bond phoned to offer me a position in South Africa. The Assembly he suggested was in Fishhoek which was not far from the Bayview Residential Nursing Home in Muizenberg where my mother was living. I believe that John Bond was trying to assist me, as he knew that I travelled down to the Cape to visit my mother every year.

Having been presented with what was an extremely attractive offer I remember praying earnestly about the situation. This took place in particular one night whilst Mally was at work. The Assembly was situated in a lovely town which I knew well. The beach was large and safe in particular for a young family and my mother would be just up the road! In addition, I had visited the Assembly on a number of occasions and knew it to be a good fellowship.

Yet, Despite this very attractive offer, I felt that I could not leave Zimbabwe, as that was where the Lord had called me. The Lord was very close to me that night and His presence very real after I had spent some time in prayer. I was persuaded that my place was still in Zimbabwe, and that I ought to reject the offer of a move. Having made up my mind, I telephoned John Bond and discovered that the Elders in Fishhoek were totally opposed to their current minister moving. As a result, I believe the Lord confirmed that I had made the correct decision and the deal fell through.

THE NATIONAL (ENGLISH LANGUAGE) WORK.

I loved being back at my home Assembly and would usually drop the boys off at school on my way to spend the morning in my office at the church. Not long after arriving in Harare, I was blessed to be able employ a secretary by the name of Marietta Bihl. On the first day that she came to work after showing her what I expected of her, I said, **"Let's pray and commit our working relationship to God."**
(My words were possibly very different but this sounds pretty good.)

After we had prayed, she told me that in all her working life it was the first time that her employer had prayed with her on her first day at work. Her work involved assisting me as the National Secretary of the National Executive, keeping the books of the National Development Fund and other things that had landed on my plate since Neil Gibbs had left. I can honestly say that without her help I could not possibly have done all that was required of me.

Occasionally, there were difficulties in one of our assemblies that required my attention, but the biggest problem was finding ministers for all of our congregations. As mentioned before, finding suitable men was a problem and I was always grateful to receive help in this area. As a result, when we needed a Minister for our congregation in Kadoma I was interested when someone mentioned an American brother who was available. He and his wife had been working in an Apostolic Faith Mission orphanage, but he was keen to get into the ministry.

Before discussing anything with him, I checked with the AFM to see if they were willing to give him a recommendation. Having been given the all clear, we had an interview and he and his wife appeared to be just what we needed. After spending some time in conversation, he enquired about the financial viability of the work in Kadoma, as he had a wife and family to support. My reply was something like this, **"It is a small Assembly and the income is not always great, but if the Assembly is not able to meet your 'salary' there is always the National Development Fund to fall back on. Just give me a ring and we will send you a cheque to meet the shortfall."**

      "How much money do you have in the National Development Fund?" He asked.

      "Let me see," I said, **"Currently we have Z\$45.00 in the fund. However, don't worry, each month money comes in and we always have sufficient."**

      I cannot remember the exact figure, but it was something like that! He must have been a man of 'faith' as he agreed to take the job!

      But in order for our American friend to be employed as a 'minister' instead of working in an Orphanage, his status in the country had to change. As a result, we were required to sign a government paper saying that, if need be, we would meet the costs of his 'repatriation' to the USA. I cannot remember all the details but he had been given a work permit to allow him to work in the orphanage, but as he was now becoming a 'minister,' we would now be responsible for his return to the USA if necessary. With around Z$45.00 in the bank, it did make me a little nervous, but maybe it showed that I was also a man of 'faith!'

Over the next few months, it appeared that everything was going well. He was well liked by the congregation and I received no negative reports. As a result, I was encouraged to believe that I had done the correct thing. But all that changed when I had a phone call from the Full Gospel Minister in Kadoma who said, **"Good morning, Pastor Robertson, this is Pastor---------, of the Full Gospel Church in Kadoma. I felt that it was important that I phone you in order to let you know what is happening in Kadoma. Do you know what your current Pastor is preaching in your Assembly?"**

I replied, "Good morning, Pastor -------. No! What is he preaching?"

"He is preaching the 'JESUS ONLY' message and has begun to re-baptise members of your congregation."

"No, I did not know that. Thank you for putting me in the picture. I will investigate this immediately," I said.

For those unfamiliar with the 'Jesus Only' message, they preach that there is only one member of the Trinity and so the name of God the Father is Jesus and the name of the Holy Spirit is Jesus. As a result, when they baptise people, they baptise in JESUS NAME, instead of baptising according to the teaching of the Lord Jesus who said,

"Go therefore and make disciples of all the nations,

baptizing them in the name of the Father and of the Son, and of the Holy Spirit." Matthew 28.19

After making a phone call to Kadoma, I set out to find out whether what I had heard was the truth. Sadly, I soon discovered that it was the truth! Not only that, but even one of the leaders of the fellowship, had been re-baptised in the name of Jesus, by our American preacher. After a conversation where I explained that it was unacceptable for 'Jesus Only' teaching to be taught in our Assembly, we arranged to meet again a few days later in Harare.

This time, when we met in Harare I was not on my own, as a couple of our ministers joined me including, John Baker and most likely Steve Bowan. After discussing the issue at length, we discovered that he was not willing to change his understanding of the Scriptures. It looked as if we had a big problem on our hands, but God was good as He had already solved the problem. Our American friend advised us that he had been in touch with a 'Jesus Only' Church in Harare who had agreed to let him work with them. I was very relieved and within days, he and his family had left Kadoma. If he had not left, we would have been faced with a very difficult situation, but God had helped me once again!

I am not sure who followed this man to Kadoma but it could well have been Steve and Linda Bowen. However, praise God, the assembly did continue and flourished and later Robbie and Fiona Burns ministered in the town. Robbie recently sent me the following in answer to a message that I had sent to him,

"I went to Christ for the Nations in '85 and was there for two years and returned to ministry in Harare with you and John Baker. I later went to Kadoma in '89 and then later we left Kadoma to go to England."

I praise God for faithful men and woman of God and that the work that we were involved with still continues to this day!

I would now like to turn to Marondera, where the Assembly had initiated a building project. They were blessed to own a large plot of land, and because their existing premises were too small, they had laid the foundations for a much bigger building. Sadly, they ran out of money when the new building was window height. This was not bad planning but due to the rapidly changing situation in the country. The building remained at window height for some years, when during the ministry of Stuart McDonald, the Town Council contacted them and said that they must either complete the building or knock it down.

They did not have the finances to complete the building so there was no alternative, it would have to come down. But, Shem Rupondo, another minister in the town, was also in the process of building a church! As a result, it was decided to extract the bricks, which must have been quite a job, and use them to finish this other church building in the local 'high density township.'

I was so blessed when I heard this story, praise God, for the fellowship of the saints! Although the one building was reduced to the 'foundation,' the building that Shem Rupondo was putting up was able to be completed. In addition, some years later, the building on that wonderful extensive foundation was finally finished! In fact, the last time I was in Zimbabwe I had the pleasure of being in the building and listening to Roland Pletts minister God's word. It is a lovely building much bigger than the old church building.

As mentioned in my second book as far back as 1972, when I first went into the ministry there was a desire to establish an independent congregation in Shurugwe, then called Selukwe. Well, this finally took place when Simon was their minister. It was a lovely congregation with some amazing people and I include a photo sent to me by Simon and Rina.

THE SHURUGWE ASSEMBLY outside the Methodist Church where they met.

While visiting Simon and Rina on one occasion, we went to see an abandoned building that was for sale.

We felt that it would be an ideal site for a Bible College. It was an enormous property that was apparently available for a very modest price. Sadly, for us it was only a dream!

Just before Simon and Rina Rhodes moved to Shurugwe in 1986, there had been a problem in the Assembly which had not been addressed. A member of the Assembly had left his wife for a short time and had an adulterous affair with another woman. The man was now back with his wife and back in fellowship behaving as if nothing had taken place. As a result, I arranged to attend the midweek meeting in Shurugwe with Simon, and asked that the man concerned be present.

When the man arrived, Simon and I took him aside and spoke to him. It soon became obvious that he was not at all 'repentant' about what he had done. When I spoke to him about the sin that he had committed he replied, **"All I can say is that my marriage has never been better since that incident."** The more we spoke to him the more we realised that there was no sense of repentance in his heart at all. I was horrified at his response to our questions, and told him that he would be placed under six months of discipline. During that time, he would not be permitted to participate in Assembly meetings. He could attend but was not allowed to pray aloud, give a testimony and so on. Once we were finished with our 'private' meeting, I advised the 'congregation' of what had taken place.

Although, at first, he appeared to accept the discipline, he did not remain in the Assembly, and was soon in fellowship with another congregation. Sadly, the minister of his new church never enquired as to his standing in the fellowship that he had just left. Let us be clear, if we are not willing to come under 'discipline' when we are in the wrong, but just leave, and find another church, the chances are that we will repeat the 'sin' that we were guilty of, in the days that are ahead.

THE 1984 CONFERENCE AT RESTHAVEN.

RESTHAVEN CONFERENCE 1984
Back row: - Pat Luffman from Youth for Christ, ?, ?, John Dunn, ?, ?, ?, Shem Ruponda.
Middle Row: - Stuart MacDonald, Steve Bowan, Robbie Burns, John Potter, Steve Bacon, AB Robertson, Willie van Rooyen, Gordon Ousterhuis, John Baker, Jeffrey Pindura, John Harrison, Andy Murlis.
Front Row: -Paul Croft, ?, Rose MacDonald, Linda Bowan, Fiona Burns, Kathy Potter, Eve Bacon, Mally Robertson, Trudi van Rooyen, ?, Sheila Baker, Clara Pindura, Claudia Harrison, ?. The children sitting on the ground included our sons Mark, Matthew and Jonathan Robertson.

In December 1984, we had a very successful Ministers' Meeting at Resthaven just outside Harare. It was truly a blessed time of ministry and fellowship with brethren from all over the country.

However, there was something that had been troubling me. When I took over the leadership of the movement from Neil Gibbs, I had been advised by John Bond to draw an allowance of around Z$100.00 a month in order to help cover my expenses. The problem was, that my fellow ministers were unaware of the allowance that I was receiving. As a result, I determined to make it known so that they could then determine whether I should continue to receive the allowance or not. Having explained it to the gathering I left the room to give them the freedom to discuss the situation.

When I returned a short while later, I was informed that not only were they happy that I received the allowance but they suggested that I should receive the equivalent of a second 'basic salary' for doing the job. In other words, whatever I was receiving as a Minister from the Assembly I should also receive from the National Development Fund.

It was a great relief to have been open with the brethren and I was amazed at the generosity that they demonstrated. But, despite their generosity, I never availed myself of the additional 'basic salary' as there always seemed to be so many demands upon our funds. Nevertheless, I want to record my thanks for their generous suggestion.

NATIONAL SECRETARY OF THE ZIMBABWE AOG.

Now, almost as soon as I had taken over the responsibility of National Secretary of the Zimbabwe AOG, I discovered a problem. The problem related to the 'Credential's Application Form' that we required prospective Ministers to complete when they applied for Credentials. As a result of what I discovered, I presented a new application form to the Executive at our next meeting. One of the things that I suggested was that all our prospective ministers made it clear that they had been married under 'The Marriage Act,' and not under the 'African Marriage Act.'

For many years in Rhodesia and now Zimbabwe, if you were a 'black' man you could get married under the African Marriages Act. This allowed the man to be married to more than one wife if he so desired. In addition, whichever 'act' a 'black' Zimbabwean was married under, the man had to provide evidence that he had paid the 'labola,' or the bride price, to the woman's parents before he could be legally married. My objection to our ministers being married under the African Marriages Act, was that it appeared that we were not opposed to our ministers being married to more than one woman!

As a result, at our next Executive Meeting it was agreed that if a man wanted to renew his credentials with the AOG in Zimbabwe, he would need to prove that he had been married under the Marriage Act, which only allowed a man to have one wife. Sadly, due to a misconception, some of our ministers never renewed their credentials from then on. The problem was, that they associated being married under 'The Marriage Act' among other things, with an expensive white wedding dress, and all that goes along with a 'white' man's wedding.

Nevertheless, one of the ministers, Jeffrey Pinduria, made plans to get married under 'The Marriage Act.' He had been married to his wife Clara for many years under the 'African Marriages Act' and they had a number of children. I agreed to perform the ceremony and assured him that it did not need to cost him anything. We could have a very simple wedding at McChlery, and all that was needed was a couple of witnesses. Having had some previous experience in taking 'marriages,' our conversation went something like this:

"Jeffrey, when is the wedding, and what time do you want it to take place?" I asked.

Jeffrey said, **"The wedding is planned for Saturday -------, at 10.00am."**

I said, **"That will be fine, but what time would you like me to arrive?"**

"You need to be here by 10.00am!" He replied.

Having heard what he had to say, I went away, but was just not able to believe what he was telling me. As a result, on the Saturday morning in question, I drove casually into the Assembly car park at five minutes to ten, never expecting to find anyone there. I was most surprised to find that they were already present and waiting for me to arrive. Jeffrey was dressed in a smart suit and Clara was looking beautiful in a flowing white gown with the children dressed up as flower girls or page boys. To my utmost surprise, almost everyone, had managed to get there on time, but not all, the only person to show up late, was the best man, and sadly he missed the wedding!

During my time as National Secretary, my responsibilities included a very distasteful job. One of the ministers, Jeremiah Kianga, a really lovely man of God, fell out with Brother Benghu and the movement that he led. As all of the church buildings were registered under the Back to God Crusade, he was told that he had to vacate the church building that he was occupying. This was particularly difficult for him as the building had been constructed a few years earlier when he was the Minister. In fact, McChlery Avenue had contributed a large sum of money to the project as we had a lot of confidence in Jeremiah as a man of God. As a result of his labour and with our assistance, a lovely church building had been constructed, and now he was being told to vacate the building that he was largely responsible for erecting.

As I have already mentioned, all our church buildings were held by local trustees on behalf of the local congregation, which was very different from the work of Brother Benghu. The problem was that all the church buildings in the work that Brother Benghu led, were owned by the Back to God Crusade under his control. Therefore, as Jeremiah Kianga had fallen out with Brother Benghu, he was required to vacate the building for someone else. Sadly, he failed to do so and that was where I came in.

As the secretary, I was asked to approach the Sheriff of the High Court in order to have him evicted. I was not at all excited about what I was being asked to do, and I had been slow to respond to their request. It was then that I received a phone call from 'the office,' in connection with this problem. The 'office' was the administrative headquarters of Brother Benghu's work in Zimbabwe. After some discussion the voice at the end of the line said, **"We do not know whether you are with us or not?"**

I was really annoyed at what he was implying and replied, **"Do you know who you are speaking to? I am the Minister of McChlery Avenue Assembly, and over the years my Assembly has contributed many thousands of dollars to the Back to God Crusade. In addition, as far as I am aware there is only one of your church buildings that we have not helped to build. In fact, right from the beginning, it was the then Minister of my Assembly that arranged for Brother Nicholas Benghu to come to Zimbabwe and we were the ones to finance his first Crusade in the country."**

Nevertheless, having had that conversation, I knew that I had to take some action. Despite my reluctance, after Jeremiah had received a written warning to vacate the building, I went with the Sheriff to the church. There was no one there when we arrived, and I watched while the locks were forced and the building broken into. But having broken into the building we discovered that someone was living in one of the rooms. This resulted in a mattress, bedding and various other possessions being unceremoniously dumped outside the building. Fortunately, these were rescued by an angry neighbour. Then, after the locks were changed, we left. I was not happy with what had been done, but it seemed that there was no other way.

The following day I was at my office when I had an angry telephone call from Jeremiah who said, **"How can you treat a brother that way?"**

To which I replied, **"You had been warned to vacate, however, you failed to respond. So, when is a brother a brother?"**

Having heard what I had to say, he slammed the phone down and a few minutes later he was at my door. He was a big man and he was angry. It was a difficult moment!!!

Not long afterwards I was asked to attend the wedding celebrations of Geoffrey Mkwanasi's daughter. One of the guests happened to be Jeremiah and I went over to speak to him. Despite what had taken place, we embraced! He truly was a really lovely man of God!

Although that was a very difficult time, there was more to come! One morning I was contacted by the wife of one of our Ministers who explained to me that her husband had been arrested by the police and detained without charge. He was being held at Chikurubi Prison, a maximum-security prison on the outskirts of Harare. He had been arrested in a government crackdown on supporters of ZAPU, and because he was Ndebele he had been targeted.

As this man was one of Benghu's ministers, I asked her if she had contacted 'the office' in Harare, the people responsible for his ministers in Zimbabwe. Her reply was that she had indeed been in contact with 'the office,' but that no help had been forthcoming. After making my own enquiries, I made an appointment with the solicitors that we had been using for property transfers and other legal issues. When I explained the situation, they advised me that they were not able to assist me as they had no expertise in that area, but were able to put me onto one of their associates. As a result of their intervention, the imprisoned Pastor was released within days, as he was being held illegally. Sadly, it is entirely possible that without our intervention, he could have remained in prison for a very a long time, imprisoned without charge and without trial.

SOME MEMORABLE WEDDINGS!

Getting back to the subject of weddings, as explained previously, all our ministers were not recognised as Marriage Officers, and so as a Marriage Officer I was often asked to officiate at weddings in other Assemblies. One day I was approached by a lovely couple, who were both leading members of an Assembly in one of the 'high density' townships in Harare. They asked if I would be willing to officiate at their wedding. I agreed, but requested that they met with me in my office at McChlery for marriage counselling, prior to the wedding.

They were a great couple, and I enjoyed our times together. But, at the last session, when I planned to speak to them about the more intimate aspects of marriage, just before the wedding, I realised that we had a problem! The lady concerned was without doubt pregnant!

When I challenged them, I was told the following sad story. The father of the bride had demanded an excessive 'bride price' and the 'labola' could not be paid. There were other problems as well, and it seemed that he would never give his blessing to the marriage. Finally, the couple decided not to wait any longer, and she was now pregnant. I have forgotten certain details of this incident but the more they explained what had transpired, the more I became sympathetic to their situation.

The following day, I was present at the appointed time, but knew that we would most likely have to wait some time before the bride arrived. While we were waiting, I was praying and meditating on what to say that day. The more I considered the situation, the more I felt that I could not just proceed as normal, I would have to say something. Finally, I went up to the groom and said, **"------, I just want to let you know that I will have to say something today about your situation."**

He turned to me and said, **"Brother, feel free to say what you have to say."**

I must make it quite clear that this couple had been 'leaders' among the young people not only in their own congregation but in all the Assemblies in the city. I could not just proceed as if all things were normal. As a result, somewhere during the service I said something like the following, **"Marriage is a very important occasion in a person's life and the Bible does not promote sex until after marriage. Marriage comes before sex, and children come after we are married not before. As Christians we need to be an example to the world around us. We are not like them; we are followers of the Lord Jesus Christ."**

I really cannot remember everything that I said that day, but I was sure that the Lord gave me the words for the occasion. As soon as I began to speak about these things the congregation came alive and I heard the people say, **"Amen! Amen brother Amen!"**

As was my norm, I did not stay for the 'reception' but I

was informed that something extraordinary took place that day. It appears that a mini revival took place, with a number of people getting right with God after I left. Although the wedding celebration continued all day, it turned out to be a time of heart searching for the Lord's people. I must stress that this couple had been totally committed to the work of the Lord and I do trust that they both went on from strength to strength, and that they brought up their children in the fear and nurture of the Lord.

Continuing with the subject of weddings, I ended up doing a number of weddings for people who were often not associated with the Assembly at all. One of these was a wedding that I took on a farm some miles outside Harare. There were a lot of people present and after the ceremony I ended up in conversation with either the best man or the groom's man and in course of conversation said, **"Are you married?"**

It was a really difficult question for him to answer! However, in reply he told me the terrible story about how his wife had died when the Air Rhodesia Viscount had been shot down some years before near Kariba. After expressing my sympathy, we enjoyed some further conversation. But before we parted, he said, **"If I ever get married again, will you be willing to come up to Kariba and perform the wedding?"**

I assured him that I would consider it a privilege, and with that we parted. And so it was, sometime later that he asked me to officiate at his wedding in Kariba. I of course agreed and Mally and I travelled to Kariba for the wedding. He was willing to put us up at the Hotel where the wedding was taking place but we asked if we could stay at a Christian Hotel which was being run by an American missionary family.

The wedding went well and I, as usual, had an opportunity to speak to a lot of unsaved people. One of the guests turned out to be a farmer and his wife who I had met in Middle Sabi. When I had spoken to him about the Lord and asked him to come to our services, he had replied something like this, **"No, I do not want to come to the services that you are taking. I do not want to get right with God as 'by hook or by crook' I plan to become a rich man!"**

It was lovely seeing him again and I took the opportunity to speak with him. Sadly, he was still far from God but whether he was 'rich' or 'poor' I did not find out.

I was really pleased to be able to perform the wedding of this dear man, who had lost his first wife in the Viscount tragedy, and after a lovely weekend we set out for home once again.

THE OUTREACH AT BEATRICE.

We were still open for business and looking for new avenues of service, despite so many of our members leaving the country, which had resulted in the closure of some of our Assemblies. One of these 'avenues of service' opened up when a young couple attended our Sunday morning service. The Wood's came from Beatrice, which was a mining and farming community 32 miles from the city. The husband worked for Joyce Mine, a medium sized gold mine and they invited us to have a meeting in their home and promised to invite their neighbours.

We enjoyed a successful meeting on that first visit, and from then on, every two weeks we had a meeting in their home. Sometimes Mally and the family came with me but on many occasions I went alone. These were great times of evangelism, teaching, and warm fellowship, with a group of around a dozen people. My piano accordion proved to be a great blessing as we enthusiastically sang many wonderful hymns and choruses. I remember an elderly couple who were members of the Dutch Reformed Church who were particularly blessed by the singing. Because things were going so well, we even tried a couple of Sunday morning services. Sadly, these failed to take off, but the regular evening meeting, every two weeks, continued to be a blessing.

When a couple in the group wanted to be baptised, we arranged to have a baptism service at the next meeting. Our eldest son had committed his life to the Lord as a five-year-old, but up and till then he had not been baptised. Each time we planned to baptise someone, he asked to be baptised, but as I felt that he was still too young I had declined to baptise him. However, at Beatrice, in a swimming pool at the Joyce Mine, Mark was finally baptised by full immersion. Sadly, the only record that we have of this very important event is a not very good photograph.

One day, we were privileged to visit the mine as a family, and receive a conducted tour. The mine was a very successful medium sized gold mine, a lot bigger, and much more up to date than the mine that I had visited as a kid. The most interesting event, which was also a little frightening, was when we all got into something like a big bucket and were lowered deep down into the mine. Sadly, I have forgotten the first name of Mr. Wood, but their enthusiasm was a real blessing to us.

Another regular couple were Andrè and Rose who had a farm in the area. They invited us to visit the farm and when we discovered that there were horses on their parents' farm nearby, we arranged to go horse riding. Andrè warned us that the horses had not been ridden for some time, but, despite that, we decided to give it a go. At the time, I was under the impression that Mark had been having riding lessons. But I learned later, that all that the lessons had involved up and till then, was being led around in a circle by someone holding the reins.

I am not sure what happened to Matthew and Mally, but I do remember what happened to Mark and myself. As soon as Mark and I were mounted, his horse set off at a fast walk, he then began to trot, and finally to gallop. I am sure that this was not entirely the horse's fault as Mark did encourage him as well, but, as soon as I was aware of what was happening, I gave chase. But I had not ridden a horse for years, and I had not gone very far when my horse decided to throw me. I managed to hold on to the reins despite being thrown, and was soon back in the saddle, much to the displeasure of the horse, and set off after Mark. As I looked ahead, I noticed to my horror that Mark was heading for a fence, or something similar, but praise God, the horse finally came to a halt. And so, after a memorable afternoon, we returned home, all in one piece, praise God!

One day Andrè and Rose presented us with a key to a cottage on their farm. They said that just as the woman of Shunem provided a room for Elisha the prophet, they wanted to provide us with somewhere to stay, whenever we were in the area. Elisha had been provided with a bed, table, chair and a lamp, and they wanted to do the same thing for us! **2 Kings 4.8-10**

However, as we so seldom travelled that way, I could not think of an occasion when we could make use of their hospitality, and so I declined their offer. Looking back on that event, I feel that I ought to have accepted their generosity and made a point of using the cottage even if it meant a special trip. We could have taken a few days off every now and then, and visited the farm, which I am sure would have been a blessing to the whole family.

Although we never made use of their hospitality in the way that they intended, we did camp on the farm, on one occasion. This took place when I took Mark, Matthew, and a few of their friends for a couple of nights camping, on the farm, which was a real blessing.

My final story about Beatrice could have had a very sad ending, but once again the Lord sent His angels to watch over me. I was travelling home at about 10.00pm one night, after another wonderful meeting with the group at the mine. On the way, I passed a group of armed men who were supposed to be guarding one of the bridges on the main road. It was then that I spotted a man frantically waving me down for a lift. I instinctively slowed down almost to a walk when my mind kicked into action. I realised that stopping to give a man a lift, on a dark night, in an isolated spot, with little passing traffic, at that hour of the night, was possibly asking for trouble. Having decided not to stop I was just pulling away when the man shouted at me, **"Please stop and help me, they are going to kill me!"**

Hearing the desperation in his voice I pulled over and he wasted no time in climbing aboard. Then just as I was pulling away, I heard a rifle shot and realised to my horror that they were shooting at me! I immediately 'put foot' and sped away as fast as I could, when another shot helped me on my way. Once we were out of harm's way, my passenger asked me to drop him off at the Police roadblock a mile or two down the road.

It was not a functioning roadblock, as I did not have to stop. It was more like a Police outpost and as soon as I stopped, my passenger got out and told the policeman on duty what had taken place. Before I went on my way the policeman turned to me and said, **"Thank you, sir, you have done a very good deed tonight."**

As I look back at what took place that evening I can only think that the Lord was watching over me as things could have turned out a lot different. Praise God that He is Lord of all! Hallelujah!

THE RESTHAVEN WOMEN'S RETREAT.

I am not sure when this took place, but it turned out to be a real blessing to the ministers' wives who attended. It came about when I was approached by a lady that I knew in the Full Gospel Church (it may well have been the Apostolic Faith Mission) who was busy arranging a special "Women's Retreat" at Resthaven. They had a special speaker from the USA and wondered whether any of our ministers' wives would be interested in attending.

I felt that it was worth supporting, and after putting the word out, a number of our ladies accepted the invitation including my own wife, Mally. Most of the ladies assembled at our home and I remember taking a carload out to Resthaven. As my passengers got out of the car, the thing that struck me, was that they all seemed to be so discouraged. Sometimes as ministers of the Gospel, we fail to appreciate the pressure that our wives are under. They, and our children, are often the target of the enemy's attack. Congregations need to pray not only for their Minister, but also for his wife and family!

It was amazing what happened in just a couple of days, as when I went to pick up my passengers, they were all filled with the joy of the Lord. Those few days had really been a blessing to all of them and I felt that we ought to organise similar events on a more regular basis. Sadly, despite what I felt, it was the only one that we ever had.

A VISIT TO THE ZIMBABWE BROADCASTING STUDIOS.

As explained elsewhere we had the privilege of being involved with the regular religious programming of the ZBC. Usually when it was my chance, and I was sitting in front of a microphone recording the Sunday morning or evening service, I would aim my messages at one man in particular. This man was Ernie Clark, the husband of Mrs. Clark who had been saved during my first stay in QueQue. I knew that he would be listening, and it was a great help to actually 'talk' to someone instead of only the official doing the recording. Praise God, before he died, I was informed that Ernie had accepted the Lord Jesus as his Lord and Saviour!

Nevertheless, on one occasion our youngest son, Jonathan, had asked if he could go with me to the studio. I had agreed provided he did not make a noise and was completely silent when we were there. As he was sitting in the studio with me, I decided to involve him in what I was doing that morning. I told my listeners that he was present, and that he had given his life to Jesus. I then turned to Jonathan and said, **"Do you love Jesus, Jonathan?"**

Sadly, my son said nothing! I had to proceed without his answer! He did love the Lord but he possibly wondered why, having been told 'possibly under pain of death,' not to say anything whilst I was recording, I now wanted him to talk?

I really praised God for the wonderful opportunities that he gave me. Hallelujah!

THE UNFINISHED TASK.

As I have already mentioned, a lot of people were leaving the country and therefore also leaving the Assembly, but praise God, we also had new people coming into fellowship. Among them were a British couple who were both teachers. In any case, although I was not fully aware of it at the time, he was also an 'undercover reporter,' sending reports overseas. These reports dealt with the terrible things that were taking place, at that time, in Matabeleland.

In any case, one day, when he and his wife were visiting our home, we talked about the need for a National AOG Magazine. After some discussion we agreed to pursue the idea and he agreed to become the Magazines first Editor. But sadly, as it turned out, before the first issue of the Magazine was ready for printing, he had already left the country.

One evening he and his wife arrived at our home with the 'unfinished,' 'UNFINISHED TASK MAGAZINE' to inform us that they were leaving for the United Kingdom the following day. He had not planned to leave as they had even purchased a house in Harare. But, as a result of information that they had received, they felt they had no alternative but to go. He had been informed that his life may well be in danger if he did not leave the country as soon as possible. The reason being, that his 'undercover' reports had finally been traced back to him.

As a result of the departure of the 'first' Editor of the Magazine, even before the 'first' issue was ready for printing, I became the Editor in Chief of THE UNFINISHED TASK. My intention was to produce a magazine that would be a blessing to the whole movement. In the first issue there was an excellent article by the 'former Editor in Chief' who had now left the country. It was based upon an incident in the history of the Kingdom of Judah, where the King refused to listen to the Prophet of God and said,

"Have we made you the king's counsellor? Cease! Why should you be killed?"
2 Chronicles 25.16

The article that he had written was a very pertinent message for all in Zimbabwe who were willing to listen!

There is no doubt that I could not have produced the Magazine without the assistance of Ken ----, who was a dear brother in Christ and a member of the Apostolic Church. He organised the typesetting and arranged the layout which included all the pictures in the magazine. Once he had it all prepared, he arranged for the magazine to be printed at very reasonable rates. He never charged for the work that he did, it was done as unto the Lord, we just paid for the printing. The end result was a very acceptable magazine, for which I could only praise God.

I am not too sure how many issues of the magazine were printed and sadly, I am no longer in possession of even one copy. If anyone reading this story has a copy of one of the issues I would be thrilled if you could send it to me or if you would rather not part with it, a photocopy of the issue would be received with thanks.

Having begun to produce the magazine, I was aware that, although by and large, we were no longer starting new congregations, (in fact we had closed two in Bulawayo, one in Harare, and one in Masvingo) God was still doing great things throughout the country. For example, I had heard that a number of new church buildings were under construction in the work being led by Brother Benghu. Having discussed these things with Rob McKenzie (one of our ministers), who possessed a pilot's license, we came up with a plan. He agreed to fly me around the country in order to take photographs of the buildings being constructed. I planned to feature them in our magazine so that our readers would be encouraged when they became aware of the ongoing work around the country. Rob was more than willing to oblige, and it may well have been his idea, as he needed to increase his flying 'hours' in order to keep his license.

On that memorable day, we flew to Gweru where a new church and conference centre was being constructed for the work under Brother Benghu's authority. We were met at the Airport by Stuart McDonald who drove us to the site, where we were shown around by Ronnie Dlamini a lovely man of God. Although building work had been suspended, due to a lack of funds, what had already been accomplished was impressive. When finished it was going to be a very large facility.

Because of Rob's assistance, we were also able to visit West Nicholson that day so that I could have a meeting with a Christian business man. Whilst living in Bulawayo he had invited me to preach at the 'house meeting' which he had arranged in the area. As a result of getting to know me, he had asked if we could make use of a large Marquee, for evangelism, that he had acquired.

The Marquee had been one of a number that had been brought into the country by the British Government during the 1980 elections. They had been used to house the combatants who were part of the ZANLA and ZIPRA forces when they came back into the country to participate in the elections. When the British packed up after the elections, they sold off a lot of surplus equipment, including the marquees. Seeing their potential for evangelism, my friend had purchased two of them and was willing to give one or both of them to us, if we were able to use them.

I believed that we could use at least one of them, to assist our brethren by providing the support that they needed to evangelise Matabeleland. As the maintenance, transport, erection, and dismantling would require some organisation, we agreed to handle that side ourselves. The plan was that we would arrange to erect and later dismantle the tent wherever it was needed by the ministers working with Brother Benghu. I discussed this plan with Brother Benghu and he gave us the go ahead. Tony Lee had agreed to take charge of the arrangements. As we considered the advantage of having this tent for evangelism, we recognised that for the project to be successful, we would also need a lighting plant and other equipment, including transport. Our visit that day was to confirm that we would proceed as planned, as soon as we were able to do so.

After a very successful meeting, it was time to set off home, however, when we returned to the plane, we were disturbed to find that one of the tyres was flat. It was vitally necessary to have both tyres at the correct pressure to take off and land. Praise God, Rob had a solution and the tyre was soon at the correct pressure and we were able to take off and land safely sometime later in Harare. I must admit it took a fair bit of 'faith' and prayer to believe that the tyre had remained pumped up for our landing at Mount Hampden Airport (now Charles Prince Airport) outside Harare.

As a result of our trip, the next issue of 'The Unfinished Task' included a number of photos of buildings that were under construction in different places around the country. But sadly, my good intentions were not appreciated by my 'brethren' as some accused me of trying to raise money for 'our work' by carrying photos of buildings under construction in 'their work!' It was really sad as the Assembly that I led in Harare had such a long history of their generous support for the 'entire work' in Zimbabwe!

Returning to Rob McKenzie, he later offered to give the whole family a short flight. As it was only a small plane, I stayed on the ground while the rest of the family took off. Having enjoyed the flight, as he was bringing the plane in to land my son, Matthew, called out, **"Can I steer?**

I had let the boys 'steer' the car when we were out at Lake MacIlwaine and Matthew felt that he could do the same while coming in to land. Naturally he never got the opportunity, I am pleased to report!

THE BIG ADVERT IN THE SUNDAY MAIL.

One day I came up with a great idea that I presented to the oversight of McChlery and then took it to the church business meeting. My idea was to take a whole page in the Sunday Mail which had National circulation to publicise our Assemblies throughout the country. In addition, I asked Ron Davies to provide a short tract from Lifeline that we could print to encourage people to get right with God. I included every Assembly in the country where we had a physical address and the business meeting at McChlery were willing to pay for the advert which was quite expensive.

I am not sure what effect the adverts had on Church attendance at our Assemblies around the country but Lifeline continued to receive replies for months after the newspaper was printed. This was very encouraging and as a result I believe that what we did was worthwhile.

However, the 'brethren' from 'the office' in Harare were not impressed and once again accused me of trying to raise money for the work under my direct control. I was saddened by their response but we were living in challenging times.

OUR LAST VISIT TO CHIPINGE.

I had a soft spot in my heart for Chipinge as so much had taken place during the time that we were there. Mike Howard, the minister who had replaced me, had since moved on and was no longer operating from Zimbabwe. He had then been replaced by Errol Lobb who had previously been one of the deacons that I had recognised before leaving the area. But Errol had also moved away and after ministering elsewhere in the country, in 1990 he and his wife and family had moved to Bindura where they pastored an independent Pentecostal Church. They successfully cared for this fellowship until 2020, when they moved to Malawi.

In 1985, the Assembly in Chipinge was being overseen by an American missionary. He was a school teacher working at Mount Selinda Methodist Mission. He and his wife were planning to be away on holiday, but there was nobody locally who was able to look after the Assembly in their absence. He asked if I could provide some covering ministry but as Chipinge is a long way from anywhere, I decided that we should go, as it would be great to visit the area again.

It was arranged that we would stay in Chipinge for two weeks living in the teacher's house on the Mission station. We would then leave early on the Monday morning, to begin our journey to Cape Town for our Christmas holiday. I praise God that we were able to do this for the last six years of my mother's life whilst she lived in a nursing home in the Cape.

As the Mission Station was right on the border of the Chirinda Forest, we made a point of paying it a visit. We never had the opportunity to go into the forest when we had lived in Chipinge as it had been far too dangerous to do 'sight-seeing.' It was really amazing on this our one and only visit to the forest, to see what is known as 'The Big Tree!' As far as I am aware it still exists and is the largest red mahogany tree in Southern Africa and considered to be hundreds of years old. Another thing that fascinated us was to see the 'parasite vines' growing up many of the trees. In fact, we saw one tree which had been completely destroyed by these 'vines' so that all that was left was the 'parasite.'

We all enjoyed our visit to the forest, as the forest protected us from the heat of the day and it was lovely and cool inside. When we prepared to leave, Matthew, one of our sons, chose to run ahead of us while we travelled on behind in the car. He really enjoyed his athletics and just wanted to do a little training!

Before leaving Harare, I obtained as much foreign currency as we were allowed, for our trip to South Africa. However, having done this, we had barely enough Zimbabwe dollars for our trip to Chipinge. However, during the time we were there we ended up doing a lot of mileage and used a lot of fuel as the distance between each member of the congregation was considerable.

As a result, when the last weekend arrived, I had become a little concerned. We had succeeded in using all the Zimbabwe dollars that we had brought with us and our petrol tank was not far off empty. But I assured the family that all was well and we would be leaving Chipinge with a full tank of petrol on the Monday morning as planned. To be quite clear I was confident that the local treasurer would make sure that I received a 'love gift' to cover some of our expenses for the time that we had been in the area, as this was the normal procedure for visiting ministers.

Anyhow, the morning dawned and after breakfast we headed for the meeting. We had a good service and spent some time saying good bye to the congregation. Finally, the treasurer waved goodbye as he drove out of the car-park without giving us the customary 'love gift!' We were the last to leave, and we now had a problem, as we needed a full tank of petrol to reach the border.

All was not lost though, as I realised that we knew the local garage owner and set out for the filling station. He was naturally not there that Sunday morning, but the attendant was willing to give me his address, which was just up the road. As a result, a few minutes later we knocked at his door and were warmly welcomed into his home. He and his wife were happy to see us and it was not long before we all had a nice cold drink in front of us.

After a decent interval, I explained what our problem was, and asked if he would cash a cheque for me so that we could fill up with fuel in order to be on our way the following morning. He was more than happy to oblige but as he went off to get the money his wife called out to him, **"----- don't cash the cheque, just give AB the money."**

They were very generous and, as a result, a short while later we were at the petrol pumps again. We had more than enough cash to fill the tank with petrol and were thus prepared for an early departure the following morning as planned. The Lord had once again been faithful in providing for all our needs.

The owner of the Filling Station said something like this to me before we left his home, **"AB, we never joined your Church, but we were very appreciative of all the work that you did here in Chipinge. We are very pleased to have been able to assist you today."**

I have always looked at those years in Chipinge as being the most productive in my entire ministry and this little incident drew attention to the fact that we not only touched the lives of those who joined the Assembly, but our little Assembly had made an impact on the entire community. We could only praise God who made it all possible!

The next morning, bright and early, we left Chipinge for good and up to the present day we have never been back. It was not many months later that the American school teacher who was leading the work in Chipinge decided to return to the USA. Sadly, we had no one who could replace him and reluctantly we were forced to close the Assembly! I remember travelling somewhere with John Baker and Stuart Macdonald when I discussed the problem with them. I said that the last thing that I wanted to do was close the Chipinge Assembly as my time there had meant so much to me. Having heard what I had to say, John replied, **"Consider it something like when Abraham was required by God to place his son Isaac on the altar of sacrifice. He was required to surrender his son to the Lord. In a similar way the Lord is calling you to lay down your 'Isaac' on the altar. You need to give Chipinge to God!"**

There was nothing that I could do, and as a result I duly laid down Chipinge, my 'son' and sadly the work was closed! It had only lasted around ten years but out of that little Assembly had come at least five and possibly more wonderfully anointed couples who went on to do exploits for the God that they served. I praise God for the chance of being associated with that fellowship and being privileged to be part of what God did in so many people's lives. Thank You, Jesus!

THE PENTECOSTAL FELLOWSHIP OF ZIMBABWE.

It was in 1985 that Glen Kauffeldt, my Canadian missionary friend, suggested that we form 'The Pentecostal Fellowship of Zimbabwe.' The idea was not to try to amalgamate the different Pentecostal 'movements' but rather to bring them into 'fellowship.' In the past, many of the 'movements' had originally worked together, but over the years they had grown increasingly isolated from one another. The idea was to renew fellowship, for the great work of the evangelisation of our country.

As I could see the benefit of such an organisation, we agreed to contact the various 'church groups' and put the proposal before them. As a result of the very good response that we received, the Pentecostal Fellowship of Zimbabwe, came into being. It included the Pentecostal Assemblies of Zimbabwe, and the Missionaries of the Pentecostal Assemblies of Canada represented by Glen Kauffeldt. In addition, it included the leaders from both sections of the Assemblies of God represented by Geoffrey Mkwanasi and myself, and both sections of the Apostolic Church. The Apostolic Faith Mission, was represented by Langton Kupara and his brother Raphael Kupara, was also involved. He had recently broken away from ZAOGA and formed his own movement but the name escapes me. Finally, there were representatives of the Full Gospel, and the Zimbabwe Assemblies of God Africa.

As is the case with any organisation, it was vital to have at least two office bearers and when a vote was taken Glen was elected as the Secretary and yours truly was elected as the Chairman. I was surprised when the result was announced and said to the mainly 'black' ministers who were present, **"How is it that you have elected a 'white Rhodesian' and a 'white Missionary' to be the leaders of this fellowship when we are now living in Zimbabwe?"**

The reply that they gave was very simple, **"We have elected you as you are the ones with the vision!"**

As a result, I remained the Chairman from 1985

until 1987/1988.

Among other things, in order to promote the PFZ, we decided to plan a Conference in Harare the following year. After some discussion, we all agreed that Reinhard Bonnke was the best person to invite to be our main speaker. As an evangelist he was making a big impact upon Zimbabwe and indeed all over the continent. At that time, there were a number of well-known preachers visiting the country. They were conducting evangelistic crusades or teaching seminars in Zimbabwe but mainly in Harare and Bulawayo. On one occasion I asked the members of the PFZ, who represented many thousands of Christians up and down the country, the following, **"Brethren, there are a number of well-known 'Evangelists' or 'Teachers' visiting our country. Many of them claim to have been used by God to perform mighty miracles of healing. Do YOU KNOW of anyone who is a member of one of your congregations who has been healed under the ministry of Reinhard Bonnke?"**

The answer was very positive and a number of testimonies were duly shared at the meeting. However, no one had a testimony to share when I mentioned the names of a couple of other men! It was clear that among the many, often 'household' names, it was only Reinhard Bonnke that we as leaders of a group of Pentecostal fellowships representing literally hundreds of congregations could with all honesty endorse!

As a result of our decision, our secretary wrote to Reinhard and invited him to minister at our Conference the following year. Sadly, the response was not encouraging, as he declined our invitation, as he had other plans.

After further discussion, we agreed to invite three different men to minister at our first conference. They were Solomon Wasker from India, Dennis White originally from the West Indies, but at that time ministering in Canada, and Mervyn Thomas a Canadian who was the pastor of the Valley Road Assembly in Nairobi, Kenya.

The venue chosen for the conference in Harare is known today as the City Sports Centre which seats around 4000 people. At the time of the Conference, Rob McKenzie was working as my assistant, more about that elsewhere, and he really saved the day. When we went to examine the premises, he asked me what I was doing about 'decorating' the place as it looked so bare. My reply was that I had not considered doing anything at all! As a result, Rob asked if he could do something about it and I willingly left it in his hands.

He contacted a friend who ran a garden centre or something similar and by the time the Conference started the platform was transformed. There were huge pot plants on the platform as well as a large banner up on the wall behind the speaker which boldly declared "JESUS CHRIST --- THE HOPE OF ZIMBABWE." Praise God for Rob, he saved the day!

The turnout was not as good as we could have hoped for, nevertheless, it was an acceptable turnout for our first conference. The weather was cold even though it was late in the year, around October, and in the evening, it was good to be wrapped up in warm clothing. As this was totally unexpected, my wife provided a warm coat for Mervyn Thomas' wife Sheila. Praise God, each of the speakers really excelled themselves, and the ministry was excellent.

Just before the first meeting began, Raphael Kupara called me over to the platform to introduce me to one of the musicians. As we were being introduced, he said, **"You remember when you preached at the tent crusade that I was holding in Shurugwe in 1971?"**

"Yes, how could I forget? It was a great privilege!" I replied.

Raphael said, **"Well this man gave his life to the Lord that night!"**

Praise God for His goodness! What a wonderful thing to be told at the beginning of these special meetings. I was really blessed by hearing this news!

One lunchtime, my wife, Mally, arranged to have Dennis White, Soloman Wasker, Glen Kauffeld, Mervyn Thomas and their wives, around for a meal. Whilst we enjoyed good food, and a lovely time of fellowship, we had the opportunity to share testimonies with one another. The testimonies of Soloman Wasker and Dennis White were very moving, as life had not always been easy, but they served the Lord despite the hardships that they had faced over the years. Part of the testimony that Dennis shared, was to do with his impeccable English. He had grown up in the Caribbean and his English was very affected by his background. However, feeling the call of God into the ministry, he made a conscious effort to learn to speak English in a way that could be understood by a wider audience. Then after a long struggle, he had succeeded and his English was, as I have already said, impeccable.

However, I will never forget the testimony shared by Mervyn and his wife Sheila. They had only just got married when they left Canada for the Mission field of Tanganyika (Tanzania.) As a result, their 'wedding presents' were still in their original packaging when they were packed away in their luggage. When they arrived at the Mission Station it was already quite late in the evening. Their neighbours, most likely other missionaries, offered to have them stay overnight at their home and they readily accepted. They left all their unpacked luggage in the house with a view to unpacking the following day.

Sadly, when they arrived the following morning, the house had been broken into, and all of their possessions had been stolen. What a start to married life and also to ministry in a foreign land?

He went on to explain that on a number of occasions their washing had been stolen from the line after they had hung it up to dry. In addition, not long after they arrived, the minister of the church, that they were pastoring together, disappeared with all the church funds. In fact, the first few years were a bit of a nightmare, but they never gave up!

Some years later they were asked to move to Nairobi in Kenya and head up the ministry at Valley Road Pentecostal Church. It was there that things began to happen and many, many people came to know the Lord as their Saviour. It was wonderful to listen to the story of how this church grew from strength to strength and very soon became one of the largest churches in the city. Despite a very difficult time, they had remained faithful and God had rewarded their faithfulness!

As I looked around our dining table, at these men and woman of God, I saw followers of Jesus who had all been tried in the fire. I knew that these were people who were worth listening to, as they had not given up, when the going had got tough.

The meetings were soon over, but we all felt that they had been very worthwhile. We may not have had Reinhard Bonnke, our first choice, as our guest speaker, but we had been privileged to have three great men of God who had all been tried in the fire. We were blessed to have had them as our guests!

CHRIST FOR ALL NATIONS.

Reinhard Bonnke and CfAN did come to Harare in 1986. In fact, I have recently discovered that the Crusade and Fire Conference had been three years in preparation. The Crusade was held over 13 days in the big tent, which seated up to 34,000 people. It coincided with the 7-day Fire Conference which was held during the daytime in the new Harare Conference Centre from the 21st -27th April 1986. The Fire Conference was attended by 4000 delegates from 60 countries, including 41 countries in Africa.

During the Fire Conference I had a phone call from the General Secretary of the British Assemblies of God who asked if I could do him a favour. A well-known minister from Nigeria was apparently attending the Fire Conference and then travelling to the UK to minster at the British AOG General Conference. The problem was that they were unsure how many were in his party and wondered if I would be able to find out and let them know.

I did as I was asked and phoned the answer through that evening. As a result of the information that I provided, a mini bus was secured to transport the Nigerian party to the conference. I later discovered that when they arrived to pick up the Nigerian party, they refused to travel in a minibus and instead demanded a Limousine to transport the 'great' man of God. His request was acted upon, nevertheless, the British were appalled and determined not to invite the Nigerian again.

We are called to be followers of the Nazarene, the one who "made Himself of no reputation!" We are disciples of Jesus, who "humbled Himself." May God help us to always remember who we are! We are not the King, Jesus is! We are not the Lord, Jesus is! No one should bow down to us, "at the name of Jesus every knee should bow, of those in heaven, and of those on earth, and of those under the earth." May God help us to give the glory to Jesus!

Although the next story is out of order as far as 'timing' is concerned, I have decided to tell the story at this time. I believe that by including it now, what happened in the Assemblies of God in Zimbabwe will be more understandable, as I will be able to concentrate on what happened one step at a time.

THE PENTECOSTAL ASSEMBLIES OF CANADA CONFERENCE. AUGUST 1986

I believe my friend Glen Kauffeld was responsible for the invitation that we received from the Pentecostal Assemblies of Canada. They invited us to attend their conference in Edmonton, Alberta, Canada from the 21st to the 26th August 1986. We were required to travel to the conference under our own steam, but, as their guests, they covered the cost of the conference and provided us with accommodation whilst we were there.

After discussing the invitation with some of the other ministers, Stuart and Rose McDonald agreed to accompany my wife and I to the conference in Canada. We were very encouraged when Mally's brother, Rod, and his wife, Fran, agreed to look after our sons in Malawi whilst we were away.

Our three sons, already had their own 'passports,' but for some reason, emergency travel documents were required for them to travel to Malawi. They were booked to travel to Lilongwe in Malawi as unescorted minors, on Air Zimbabwe. Mark was not quite 11, Matthew was 9 and Jonathan was only 7 years old.

You may find it hard to believe what I must now tell you, but sadly it is true! Although they naturally knew that they were going to spend some time with Uncle Rod and Aunty Fran in Malawi, they did not know, or had forgotten their uncle's surname! But that was not all, we sadly failed to give them a phone number or the address where they would be staying. As a result, when the flight was diverted to Blantyre due to bad weather, it could have been a big problem, as it is nearly 200 miles from Lilongwe. But God was good to us as always, and Rod and Fran picked them up at the airport without too many problems.

The boys had a lovely time in Malawi, and it was really very kind of my brother-in-law and his wife to have them. But, whilst they were there, two incidents happened that are worth mentioning, and the first could have caused major problems.

One day while they were playing in the garden, they mistook the telephone line for a 'foefie slide' and proceeded to use it as such. When their uncle and aunt saw what was happening, they were not impressed, to say the least! Getting the telephone fixed in Malawi could take months! The next incident had a much happier ending. They were entered in a 'Mountain Bike' race and Matthew came first in his age group. Praise God, their visit to Malawi was a real blessing to them all.

As usual 'foreign currency' was a problem, as due to the number of trips that had been made across the border to South Africa, most of our allowance for the year had already been used. Knowing the situation, my friend Glen offered to loan me some Canadian Dollars which helped tremendously. The arrangement was that I would pay him back in Zimbabwe Dollars on our return. As it happened when we returned, he told me not to pay him back as the money was a gift. Praise God for his generosity!

We flew to England and were met at the airport by Nelson Hogg a member of Ray Belfield's congregation. Once he had greeted us, he handed us the keys of the car that we had hired from him. As a result, we were soon travelling up the motorway heading for Wigan in the North West of England. It turned out to be a very busy week as Ray had arranged a number of meetings for us starting in Wigan. We visited a number of different congregations, who graciously provided us with accommodation, and Stuart and I shared the ministry.

Among the assemblies we visited were Wigan, Leicester, and Bethshan in Manchester. It was a great experience and a wonderful week. As we travelled from place to place, we were able to see something of the beautiful, British countryside. Once again the Lord was gracious in providing for us through the 'love gifts' that we received. After paying for the hire of the car and the fuel to get us around, the few extra pounds that we were left with, greatly assisted our financial situation when we left for Canada.

After an uneventful journey, we landed safely in Toronto. There we were met by Rev. Cornelius the Director of Overseas Missions at the very busy terminal. He did not know what we looked like but I was the very first person that he approached when he said, **"Hello, are you Brother Robertson by any chance?"**

With literally hundreds of people milling around it was really amazing that I was the first person that he approached. He and his wife, and indeed all the Canadians that we met, could not have treated us with more kindness. They took us out for lovely meals and showed us around their headquarters in Toronto which were then situated at 10 Overlea Boulevard. We were amazed to discover that almost all of the staff had spent time in Zimbabwe. One man said that he had attended Umtali Boys High and a lady said that she had gone to Umtali Girls High School. The contact with Zimbabwe was amazing and we were very impressed by what we were shown.

That Sunday they were kind enough to take us to two different Churches. As we sat down in a large Church for the morning service, I turned around to Mally and said, **"I can assure you that we will not see anyone that we know at this morning's service."**

Invariably when we attended a Church in South

Africa, we would spot someone we knew from Zimbabwe. But here in Toronto, ------- it would be unlikely that we would see anyone that we knew. Yet, the words were hardly out of my mouth when a couple sat down behind us and a voice said, **"Hello, AB, what are you doing here?"**

Amazingly, only a few days before, I had met the man who addressed me in Harare!

That evening we were taken to another Church. It was newly built and had seating for over a thousand people. That evening, in the height of Summer, there were only a few hundred people present and the huge auditorium looked quite empty. The building was magnificent and no expense had been spared in its construction. After the service, when we were shown around, I noted that they appeared to have a Grand Piano in every room. There were many different rooms around the vast building catering for the Sunday School, the Youth, a Prayer Room, and so on. We were very impressed with the luxury of the building as even in the minister's office the carpet was inches deep!

The man who showed us around was the person leading the service that evening. Sadly, he had managed to pick hymns and songs that nobody seemed to know. In addition, the guest singer was a great disappointment, and really almost everything seemed to have gone wrong. In fact, he confessed to us afterwards that he was tempted to say to the congregation, **"Let us just go home, hopefully, next week I will do better."**

Strangely I was very encouraged by what happened that night. I realised that no matter how much we try for 'perfection,' unless God shows up, we will fail! That church building had everything, however, that evening, nothing happened. Perhaps the Lord was saying that whatever they had, without HIM, it would all come to nothing.

Before leaving Zimbabwe, the Director of Missions had phoned me and asked if there was anything that we wanted to see whilst in Toronto? I had replied that we would love to see Niagara Falls not knowing just how far away from Toronto it actually was. He promised to see what he could do and while we were in Toronto, he asked his secretary to use his car and take the four of us, on a day trip to the falls.

It was a fabulous day out and the Falls are really lovely, not as magnificent as the Victoria Falls but nevertheless very impressive. We even went on a boat called the 'Maid of the Mist' which took us very close to the actual 'falls.' We were so close that, but for the rain coats that they had provided, we would have all been soaked.

Some years before, Doug and Felicity Robertson had moved to Canada from Zimbabwe. They were now living in a flat in a huge tower-block in Toronto. Ray Roberts and his wife, Felicity's sister, had also moved from Zimbabwe to Canada and were living in an adjacent tower-block. We had arranged to spend the week in Doug and Felicity's flat whilst they were away in Europe. They had left the keys with our hosts with instructions of what was what, and also the phone number of Ray Roberts and his wife. However, because of all that was going on, we had yet to make contact with them.

However, on the Monday, after visiting the headquarters of the PAOC, our hosts took us to lunch at a particular restaurant. We had just sat down and were beginning to eat our food when we overheard a lady on the opposite side of the room say to her friend, **"We do not know whether they have arrived as we have not heard from them. They should have arrived on Saturday. They are supposed to be staying in Doug and Felicity's apartment, whilst they are away."**

As a result of what I overheard, I went over to their table and introduced myself. It was really amazing that in a city the size of Toronto we ended up in the same restaurant. We had a lovely visit to their home which we were able to reach by walking from our car park to their car park, underground, and then taking the lift up to their floor. We were told that it was a great blessing in the winter, to be able to avoid the deep snow outside.

Whilst we were in Toronto, we were able to visit the CN Tower which at 1,815 feet tall (553 metres) was the tallest tower in the world, from when it first opened in 1976 until 2007. We caught a lift up to the observation platform where the views were spectacular. You could ascend a flight of stairs a bit higher if you wished, but that was not for me, as it was scary enough, where we were. I ought to have encouraged Mally to go with Stu and Rose who were brave enough to ascend as far as they could, as she was quite comfortable with the height, but I was not willing to go any higher.

After a number of eventful days in Toronto, we flew to Vancouver where we stayed with a dear brother who had been a missionary in the Congo with the Congo Evangelistic Mission (CEM.) He and his family had fled the Congo in the '60s and had settled in

Bulawayo where he had been an Elder at Bethshan Tabernacle. When things began to change in Rhodesia, they decided that once was enough, and arranged to leave the country. They had no desire to flee for their lives a second time! They moved back to England and then on to Canada where they settled. They were now living in Vancouver, where he was one of the ministers in a large church.

Whilst in Vancouver we had the privilege of going to the Canadian National Exhibition or Expo '86, the World's Fair. The venue was enormous and the 'line up's' or queues for most of the exhibits were incredibly long. We only had limited time, and so we tended to head for the shorter 'line ups' as the Canadians called them. Once again it was such a privilege to have had this opportunity.

My mother's brother lived in Victoria on Vancouver Island and we took the opportunity to spend a couple of days with him. We took the ferry across from Vancouver to the Island where he met us and took us to his wonderful home. It was great to meet him and he was very good to us, taking us to see another relative, my mother's sister, Mabel, and her husband who also lived on Vancouver Island but some miles away. But the time was soon over and we had to be on our way once more.

Our next stop was Edmonton in Alberta, where we attended the conference which was the main reason for our visit to Canada. I believe that we must have purchased a ticket which enabled us to visit Toronto, Vancouver and Edmonton for a very reasonable price, as we would not have made these visits if it had meant spending a lot of extra cash. I also believe that Glen, my missionary friend, managed to get us a good deal with the airlines.

On arrival in Edmonton, our host was there to meet us and they could not have been kinder. They showed us around this 'oil' rich city, which among other things had a huge artificial waterfall which looked similar to the Niagara Falls. They also took us to the West Edmonton Shopping Mall, which is the largest shopping mall in North America. When we arrived at the shopping mall, as Mally was looking forward to having a coffee she said, **"Will there be somewhere where we can get something to drink?"**

You need to remember we were from Zimbabwe; how could we know that there are over 40 restaurants inside the place!! It was enormous, and quite an experience to visit. Our hosts really looked after us, for which we were extremely grateful, but more of that later.

The conference was a real blessing and we enjoyed some great ministry during our time there. One of the things that I really appreciated was how the 'older ministers' were honoured. In our work in Zimbabwe, we were nearly all 'younger' men and so we had precious few 'older' men to honour, so it was a real eye opener to see how the conference 'honoured' the older men and women of God. It is something that the younger ministers need to take note of as usually you will be building on the foundation laid by those who have gone before. The work that you are able to do is usually only because others have gone before and opened the way!

In any case, we found the conference much like

the West Edmonton Mall, it was rather overwhelming! The abundance of books, Sunday school helps, Christian magazines, and other literature, was amazing. I would have loved to have been able to pack a suitcase full of all the resources available, but it was not possible!

The Missionary Meeting on the Sunday afternoon was without doubt the highlight of the conference for all of us. This was held in an amazing venue that was specifically secured for the occasion. We found ourselves seated towards the back of the building; a little bit higher than the main seating area. The Pentecostal Assemblies of Canada have an amazing missionary programme. They are currently involved in 65 countries! One of the highlights of the afternoon took place when representatives of each of these countries entered the auditorium, carrying their national flag.

As it happened, we could have been sitting anywhere in the auditorium that afternoon. However, when the group accompanying the Zimbabwe flag stopped, at their designated position, they were immediately in front of where we were sitting! People were then asked to join the flag bearers and those accompanying them to pray for the country represented. We immediately left our seats and assembled around our flag and prayed for Zimbabwe.

Up until then I was indifferent to the Zimbabwe flag preferring the green Rhodesian flag which I missed. Nevertheless, that day there were tears in my eyes, as I prayed with others for my homeland around the flag of Zimbabwe. This made the missionary meeting that

Sunday afternoon even more special and brought this wonderful conference to a dramatic conclusion!

Moving on from there, one evening whilst we were staying with our Canadian hosts, shortly before we left, I sat down at their piano and was just tinkling the ivories when the man of the house said, **"I did not know that you played the piano?"**

I replied, **"I don't really, my wife plays more than me, my instrument is really the piano accordion."**

Having made that remark, it was only a few minutes later, when he appeared with a lovely red piano accordion. It was almost new, but had not been used for years. Anyhow, these kind people presented this lovely piano accordion to me as a gift before we left, to take home with us to Zimbabwe. Once again, the Lord had truly blessed us!

It turned out that our host had a PC or personal computer which was stored in the basement. He explained that it had been all the rage a couple of years before, but now most people were not bothering with them. He said that it appeared to him that the craze to have a PC was now well and truly over! He was a lovely man, but how wrong could he have been? The PC in its various forms, including the laptop, and the smartphone have taken over the world since that time!

My sister and her husband had sold their wonderful fruit farm in Juliesdale in the highlands of Zimbabwe and emigrated to Canada some years before. They were now living in Summerland in British Columbia which was nearly 600 miles from Edmonton. Despite being relatively 'so close,' it did not seem as if it were possible to visit them. But all was not lost as our hosts arranged for friends of theirs, to give us a lift. Their journey home after attending the conference, would take them close to where my sister was living.

But that was not all, as our excellent hosts encouraged our driver to take a deviation whilst crossing the Canadian Rockies and show us the Athabasca Glacier. This proved to be an experience that we would never forget. We spent a short while walking on the glacier and were able to see just how far it had receded in recent years. The Rockies and the glacier revealed the majesty of Almighty God but the railway through the Rockies revealed the ingenuity of man. The construction of the railway is an amazing story. We were able to see a train disappear down a tunnel and emerge from that same tunnel higher up the mountain doubling back upon itself. They had constructed a spiral tunnel which was an amazing spectacle to behold.

Some hours later, our kind friends dropped us off in Kamloops which was a couple of hours drive from where my sister and her family were living. Praise God, they were there to meet us! It was great to see the family as it had been some years since we had met. However, it was only a fleeting visit and, on our return, my brother-in-law Patrick, gave us a lift back over the Rockies to Calgary, where he was working at the time. We then boarded a Greyhound Bus to Edmonton. After staying another night with our hosts, they saw us to the airport where we caught our plane back to Toronto.

During our short stay in Summerland we visited a travel agent to confirm our flight home. They informed us that if we caught the flight that we were booked on, we would arrive too late in Toronto to catch our connecting flight back to Amsterdam. The lady we spoke to altered our booking and put us on a flight that stopped at all the state airports across the country before reaching Toronto. The flight would last all day but we would arrive in time for our connection.

We flew from Edmonton to Calgary which was also in Alberta, then to Regina in Saskatchewan, then on to Winnipeg in Manitoba and finally on to Toronto in Ontario. Each journey lasted between an hour and an hour and a half and if we did not know how large Canada was before, we truly understood it's size after that flight. It is enormous!

As it turned out, we had plenty of time to change terminals as our next flight was delayed by three hours or more! As a result, when we finally landed in Amsterdam our flight to Harare had long since departed. This could prove to be a problem as our sons were returning from Malawi and it was possible that we would not be there to meet them. But, the Lord had it under control, and we were booked on a flight to London, where we caught a direct flight to Harare arriving earlier than we would have, had we been on the original flight. We were home, and it was great to meet up with our adorable sons on their return from an eventful trip to Malawi.

Having spoken about our trip to Canada we will now examine what took place during the two years before, including what took place at our own much more modest conference in Zimbabwe.

THE 1985 NATIONAL CONFERENCE.

The 1985 Conference, was held at the Baptist Seminary campsite outside Gweru. The 'ministry' was excellent and was well received and despite there being a few difficulties the whole event was a success. Sadly, as is the case at most 'conferences,' many of the delegates had already left to return home before the final meeting. Yet, those who remained to the end, were really blessed when after the final meeting Paul Croft led us in a wonderful 'singsong' on his guitar. The 1985 Conference had really ended on a high note for which we praised God!

After the last song, we all headed for bed and that night I had a very vivid dream. It was so vivid that as soon as I could the next morning, I shared it with the ministers who shared our dormitory. I was sure that God had spoken, and knew that I had to do something about what he had shown me. The problem was, I was not sure what I should do? The following is a record of my dream,

"I dreamed that I was standing on a bridge most likely crossing a river, however, I did not at that time see any water. It was a solid bridge similar to many that could be found all around the country. There were a lot of people on the bridge with me, but I did not notice any cars or other vehicles.

As I looked out from the bridge, I saw another bridge that looked like Tower Bridge in London. It was standing further upstream from where we were standing but as I looked, I was amazed to see that the 'draw bridge' was behaving very erratically. I could see that it was moving up and down more

and more rapidly, causing the whole structure to begin to fall apart. My first inclination was to run. The collapse of the bridge, not far from where we were standing, was going to have a major impact on our bridge and possibly lead to it collapsing as well. But I was very aware that if I ran, it would most likely cause people to panic, and so I gripped onto the rail on the side of the bridge, and waited to see what would happen.

I did not have long to wait as what looked like Tower Bridge, soon collapsed, and the whole structure fell into the water. When the two Towers and the rest of the bridge hit the water, it caused what looked like a Tsunami. The 'tsunami' of water that headed towards the bridge that I was standing on caused it to be severely damaged. It was so badly damaged that it also began to collapse. As it started to go down with me hanging on to the railing the dream came to an end."

When I shared my dream with my fellow ministers the following morning, they all agreed that it must be from the Lord. In fact, our guest speaker who was still present said that as far as he was concerned the two 'towers' represented Brother Bond and Brother Benghu. Although I could see where he was coming from, I was not sure what it meant, or what I should do, or indeed whether I should do anything at all. Nevertheless, I requested that all the recently elected 'English Language' Executive members meet with me the following week in Harare.

After I had spent some time praying and meditating upon my 'dream,' I was convinced that we had to act swiftly. As a result, when we met the following week in Harare, I proposed the following: -

1) THE ENGLISH LANGUAGE WORK MUST BE UNITED!

I truly believed that we could not afford any division in the work if we were to survive. We had to walk in unity! In addition, I firmly believed that,

2) THE ASSEMBLIES OF GOD IN ZIMBABWE MUST BE ONE WORK!

As things stood there were two very separate works, brother Benghu's and Brother Bond's. I believed that in Zimbabwe it needed to be ONE WORK and not two. After a lot of discussion, it was clear that the Executive members were willing to support me in what I proposed, although I am sure that there was a fair bit of apprehension. After the meeting, I took Gary Smith, to the airport to fly home to Bulawayo before going home myself. When I walked into our home, I discovered Rob and Leslie La Grange, sitting in our living room talking with my wife. Rob, one of our credentialed workers, was ministering at Resthaven to an independent congregation. I cannot remember his exact words but it was something like this, **"AB, I need backing, I cannot work as an independent."**

I am sure that those were not his exact words but it was something similar. I was amazed, as Rob was one of the men that I was planning to visit. I had planned to encourage him to work more closely with the rest of the AOG ministers. It was an amazing confirmation that I was on the correct path. In the following days, I made a point of visiting men like Steve Bacon, and others to seek to draw the fellowship closer together however, sadly, as I am writing this account, I am not sure that we really provided the support that Rob and Leslie needed at that time.

In addition to trying to draw the local fellowships closer together, I also contacted John Bond in South Africa and requested a meeting as soon as possible. Not long afterwards, I shared with him and others what I felt the Lord had shown me. I was given a fair hearing when I stressed that we needed to have 'one' AOG in Zimbabwe, and that we should offer to place all the former 'white' churches under the leadership of Brother Benghu. Having heard what I had to say Brother Bond told me that he felt that this would be unacceptable to Brother Benghu, however, he suggested that I speak to the man himself.

It was decided that I should attend the upcoming South African General Conference where I would be able to put my proposal directly to brother Benghu. It was a real privilege to attend the South African Conference at the new 'Back to God Crusade' Conference Centre at Thaba Nchu. The building was enormous and accommodated many thousands. When you stood at the back of the building the preacher appeared very small despite standing on the six foot high platform. The roof was so large that when it rained the water running off the roof threatened to undermine the foundations. It was an amazing achievement for the work under the leadership of Brother Benghu.

When I met up with Brother Benghu before I shared my dream, I made it quite clear, that having 'prophetic dreams' was not something that I was accustomed to have, and that was why I felt that it was so significant. He listened patiently when I shared my dream with him, and also gave me time to share what I felt we ought to do. He then said, **"Brother Bond and I work as one, I see no reason for us to change."**

It was quite clear that he was not prepared to allow the 'English language' churches to join up with the fellowships under his control. Although I was disappointed by his reply, I felt that I had done what I was required to do. I had shown by my actions that we were willing to change, but he was not willing to alter the existing situation. The fact is, that our administration was so different to his, that it would not really have been possible for us to come together as one single work.

As an example, the 'white' assemblies although generally 'wealthier' would not find it possible to raise the finances to build a conference centre anywhere near the size of the one at Thaba Nchu. Each Assembly was autonomous, owned its own buildings, and paid its own minister. These congregations would not be happy to spend a lot of money on a building that was a long way from home and which would not be used very often. The 'Back to God Crusade' operated in a very different way and as a result, despite the individual Assemblies being 'poorer,' it was much easier to raise the relevant funds from the hundreds and hundreds of congregations right around the country in order to build a massive centre.

Having fulfilled part of what I felt led of the Lord to do, I returned home. Despite Brother's Benghu and Bond being unwilling to change, things changed very rapidly from that time onwards.

1985 MINISTERS MEETING HELD AT TRIANGLE.

It must have been the result of a desire to forge a greater unity in the work, that we arranged to have a 'Ministers' Meeting' in Triangle in 1985. The town served the workers of the big Sugar Estates in the area, and the Assembly had been established to meet the spiritual needs of the people. I was really encouraged to visit and see the wonderful work that Jannie Nel, and his wife were doing in the area.

At the time, we were privileged to have Dave and Maureen Onions visiting from South Africa. They had also been part of McChlery Assembly in Harare in the past and were both powerfully anointed by the

Holy Spirit. Whilst they were in the country, I loaned Dave and Maureen my 'church' car enabling them to visit a number of our Assemblies up and down the country. We had a great time of ministry with a number of Ministers in attendance.

TRIANGLE MEETING.
Top row from left to right: - Dave Onions, Willie Van Rooyen, Gordon Ousterhuis, Stuart McDonald, Jannie Nel, Gary Smith, -----, Paul Croft, Steve and Linda Bowen. Bottom row: -AB Robertson, John Harrison, John Baker, John Potter, Andy Murlis. My apologies for those whose names escape me at the time of writing.

At the end of the gathering I was encouraged to believe

that we had been drawn closer together in the wonderful work of proclaiming the Gospel to our nation.

TROUBLE AHEAD.

Sometime in the middle to late 1970s, a bi-annual meeting was started by Brother Bond at CYARA for those ministers and leaders working with him. This camp site / conference facility was most likely operated by Youth for Christ. This mini conference enabled all those working with him to meet in between the South African General Conferences for fellowship and ministry. We were given special treatment by the South Africans and did not have to pay for the conference, because of the foreign currency constraints that we were under in Zimbabwe. But we did of course have to use foreign currency, in order to get to and from the meetings.

At one of those gatherings, I was given the opportunity to speak about the work in Zimbabwe and I took the opportunity to mention a number of things. First of all, I spoke about the exodus of ministers leaving Zimbabwe for South Africa and asked the conference why it was that no South Africans had been called by God to come North? I also mentioned how hard it was to get certain things in the country, which were easily available to those living in South Africa.

My ministry that day resulted in a number of comments and reactions. The first one came from one of the South African ministers who said, **"I really hope that God does not call me to Zimbabwe!"**

The second came from Ray Belfield, a guest from

the UK, who I knew quite well. He said, **"Abe, had I been leading that meeting, I would have immediately taken up an offering for the work in Zimbabwe!"**

I appreciated his comments and would have been very grateful had something like that taken place.

The last comment, which, unlike the first two, resulted in action! The 'action' came from Sonia Botha, a lady who was working amongst the Chinese people of South Africa. Some years before, she had started a Nursery School looking after their children feeling that the Lord had laid it on her heart to reach out to the Chinese. Over the years this had resulted in the development of a wonderful work, reaching many Chinese people in the country. From that nursery had come many converts which ultimately led to the establishment of a Chinese Church with a Chinese Pastor! Praise God!

However, having listened to what I had to say, she decided to bless us with parcels of goodies, including chocolates for my children, which she sent to us in Zimbabwe. We received the parcels, which were a real blessing to us and knew that they came to us from members of her Chinese congregation with the love of Jesus. Sadly, instead of receiving this gift from the Lord, I felt that the needs of the people giving to us, were greater than ours. As a result, I suggested that there were many more worthy causes for their generosity than ourselves.

Looking back, I realise that I was wrong, as my family were constantly having to sacrifice and God had provided a real blessing for them which I rejected. All my Christian life I have believed that it is vital, as followers of Jesus, that we are not to seek riches for ourselves. But sometimes I have forgotten that when God reaches out to give, we should be happy to receive!

Now, let me make it clear that ever since I had taken on the leadership of the work in Zimbabwe, under John Bond, I had enjoyed a very good relationship with him. Somewhere around this time, just before we left to return to Zimbabwe by plane, Brother Bond asked whether we needed anything. As a result of his generosity, we ended up returning to Zimbabwe with a new vacuum cleaner. Sadly, the vacuum cleaner was confiscated when we went through customs, as the 'value' of the machine was more than the two of us were allowed to bring back into the country!

I was really annoyed that this 'gift' had been confiscated, and tried everything I could to retrieve what we had been given. Finally, the customs officer came up with a suggestion. He said that I could pick up the machine and return it to South Africa, and provided the whole family were together we could then bring it back to Zimbabwe. With the five of us together the value of the machine would not exceed our allowance. We could then bring the vacuum cleaner back into Zimbabwe and finally enjoy our 'gift.'

We must have been living in Bulawayo at the time as we took a trip down to Tshipise. This was a 'hot springs' resort, not far from Beit Bridge on the border of South Africa. After an enjoyable couple of nights at this amazing resort we returned to Bulawayo with our 'gift.'

It was on one of those wonderful occasions at Cyara that a woman I knew told me that she had something to share with me. As a young woman Margaret (Pratt) had played an important role in my coming to Christ. She had matured into a wonderful woman of God and was now married to one of the ministers attending the conference. The following is basically what she had to say, **"The other night I had a dream and I saw a tree that had a very slender trunk. Despite the trunk being so very slender the branches of the tree were spread over a huge area. In fact, I saw that the branches were spread over an entire country. The Lord showed me that the tree was you and the country was Zimbabwe!"**

We did not talk much about the dream but I was quite sure that what she had revealed to me was very accurate. The question was whether I would be able to strengthen the trunk and continue to have an influence over the entire country?

Not only did I have a good relationship with John Bond, I am quite sure that my relationship with Nicholas Benghu was equally as good. In order to maintain and strengthen that relationship, I made a point of visiting him whenever he was in Bulawayo, or Harare. Although there were always people waiting to see him, whenever I arrived, after a few minutes at the most, I would be invited in to see him. In fact, it was only as a result of this good relationship, that he had agreed to us working with his men in Matabeleland on tent missions among other things.

Despite this, one day in 1984, completely out of the blue, I was informed that Brother Benghu refused to see me. No matter how hard I tried, I met with a brick wall, and I was offered no explanation. Then finally, I was advised that until 'this issue,' was resolved, he would not meet with me. Yet, no matter how hard I tried, no one was prepared to inform me, what the 'issue' was all about.

At that exact time, I received a letter completely out of the blue, from Keith Cantrell in South Africa. He and his wife Gaille had moved to South Africa from Harare some time before. They were now ministering with the Coastal Assemblies under Mike Attlee. The letter that I received from Keith was a great encouragement. In his letter he quoted what God had said to Jeremiah many years before,

"Therefore, prepare yourself and arise, and speak to them all that I command you. Do not be dismayed before their faces, lest I dismay you before them. For behold, I have made you this day a fortified city and an iron pillar, and bronze walls against the whole land---- against the kings of Judah, against its princes, against its priests, and against the people of the land. They will fight against you, but they shall not prevail against you, for I am with you," says the Lord, "to deliver you." Jeremiah 1.17-19

I cannot tell just how much it meant to me to receive this letter at this time of 'crisis!' Despite Keith being many miles away, he had written a letter that was a real encouragement to me and that I am positive was from the Lord!

It needs to be understood that most of our ministers, although leading mainly 'white' congregations, were doing their best to reach out to the rest of the population in Zimbabwe. They were often working with the 'black' ministers in their area. We were all keen to assist our brethren in reaching out to the whole community, whoever they were. As an example, John and Claudia Harrison excelled in this work in the Umtali area using their contacts with the many farmers in the area. They arranged for one particular minister to have access to the farm workers, resulting in many getting saved. Their assistance involved liaising with the farmer, transport and financial support.

One day, John was asked by the minister who was working with him in the area to cash a cheque. The minister concerned had received this 'cheque' from the 'Back to God Crusade' in Harare. All the time that John had been working with this man, he had been paying him a 'wage,' unaware that he was one of Brother Benghu's ministers, and being supported by his office in Harare. When John realised who had issued the cheque, he responded by saying something like this, **"I am not going to continue to support one of Benghu's ministers."**

He was annoyed that the man had in effect been receiving 'two wages' and was no longer willing to continue. He should also have been aware of Brother Benghu's request that none of his ministers should be supported by the 'white' churches and that all support ought to be through the Back to God 'office' in Harare.

Nevertheless, this turned out to be the 'issue' that Brother Benghu was referring to but it was several weeks before I knew what it was. The message that had been relayed to Harare, was that one of the men working with me, John Harrison, was not prepared to work with Brother Benghu. This sadly resulted in everything that we had been planning, coming to an end. The Tent Crusades would never take place, much to our regret, and the growing cooperation that had been taking place around the country, would end.

As a result of this 'issue', a meeting was called which was attended by Brother's Benghu and Bond from South Africa. Among other things it was made clear that any 'black' congregations that we were leading, must come under the leadership of Brother Benghu. This was despite them being held in our Assembly buildings, and being run under our authority. As the man who was responsible, under Brother Bond, for our Assemblies, I reluctantly had to agree. However, I was far from happy and I believe that this meeting was largely the cause of what took place later.

When I presented the 'news' to the Sunday afternoon 'Shona' congregation, they were not at all happy. They were happy to continue under my leadership, but were not going to join up with the work being led by Brother Benghu. Because I insisted that we could not continue as before, they stopped meeting at McChlery and I later learned that Steve Bacon had allowed the whole group to relocate to the premises that he was occupying in Harare.

The McChlery 'Shona' congregation was not the only 'Shona' meeting taking place in our church buildings around the country. I naturally did not enquire how many were taking place as I was not happy with the decision that had been forced upon me. But there was one meeting taking place in our Hatfield Assembly that I definitely knew about. When I spoke to Philip Chigome in Hatfield, he pleaded with me not to change things, and I agreed to leave it for the time being. Philip continued on at Hatfield as the minister running a multi racial 'English' language fellowship and a 'Shona' service on Sunday afternoons, much like we had previously been doing at McChlery.

As I write my story, I wonder whether I had truly taken in the words that God spoke to Jeremiah so long ago. Perhaps the message that I received from Keith Cantrell was in order to encourage me to resist the demands of Brother's Benghu and Bond. It is possible that I ought to have just said 'No!'

"Therefore, prepare yourself and arise, and speak to them all that I command you. Do not be dismayed before their faces, lest I dismay you before them. For behold, I have made you this day a fortified city and an iron pillar, and bronze walls against the whole land---- against the kings of Judah, against its princes, against its priests, and against the people of the land. They will fight against you, but they shall not prevail against you, for I am with you," says the Lord, "to deliver you." Jeremiah 1.17-19

MEMORIAL SERVICE IN PIETERMARITZBURG.

None of us live forever in this world, and it was sometime in 1985 that we learned of the death of Brother Benghu, who died at the age of 75 in Cape Town. During his lifetime, he had been a giant in the faith, and under his able leadership over 2000 churches had been established across Southern Africa. A carload of us travelled down to Pietermaritzburg, to what we understood was to be his funeral. In addition to ourselves, I believe that at least one and possibly two coach loads of people also travelled down from

Bulawayo and Harare.

The 'funeral' was held in a large stadium which accommodated thousands of people. But when the huge crowd were all seated, we were in for a surprise! Before he died Brother Benghu had given very specific instructions about his 'funeral.' In fact, his actual 'funeral' had already taken place sometime before, only a few days after his death. What we were attending was only a memorial service, and in accordance with his instructions there would be no eulogies. The choir would sing, and a message would be preached, and that would be that! He had lived his life to honour the Lord and he was not going to allow his funeral to change that.

It was an amazing occasion and I was privileged to have been able to attend.

DEVELOPMENTS AT McCHLERY.

For years this Assembly had been the driving force behind the development of much of the 'work' in Zimbabwe. I was their 'senior' minister, but in one way or another I was often involved with the National work. In addition, my secretary was mainly involved in the 'national' work and so I could go on. But I should have realised that things could not continue the way they were, when the following incident took place.

I had asked Rob McKenzie to work with me and I wanted to provide an office for him at McChlery. He was living out at Resthaven which was some distance from town, and so he would need an office at the church if he was to assist me in any meaningful way. Sadly, this was one step too far for my Elders and an office was not made available, resulting in Rob becoming my assistant from afar!

He was a very talented man and it was a real blessing to have him work with me. He was writing a book at the time, which was published in 1986 under the title, **'BANDS, BOPPERS, AND BELIEVERS.'** The book dealt with the evil influence of much of modern music upon Christian and non-Christian young people and is really worth reading. I asked him preach on the subject at McChlery one Sunday evening as I felt that it was such an important subject. He told me later that ours was the very first church to give him that opportunity. However, during the following years he spoke in many different churches, including, 'DIE GROOTE KERK' in Cape Town, the oldest place of Christian worship in South Africa and one of the main Dutch Reformed Churches in the country.

Sometime later Rob also wrote a book on the life of David Livingstone, a man that he greatly admired. The book was called '**David Livingstone: The Truth Behind the Legend**,' and was published in 1993. This is another book that is really worth reading and I recommend it to you.

One day Rob, my assistant from afar, came to see me. He told me that a Christian friend of his had been asked to produce a series of half hour TV programmes for the Zimbabwe Broadcasting Corporation. The programmes were to focus on organisations like 'THE LEPROSY MISSION,' 'THE SALVATION ARMY,' and 'THE RED CROSS,' showing how the Christian Church had been a blessing to the entire country. But his friend needed his help, and Rob asked if I would release him so that he could assist him. As it was such a wonderful opportunity, I willingly gave him my blessing to assist in the production of these TV documentaries. Sadly, for reasons that I have never discovered, it was only a few days later that Rob informed me, that his friend had abandoned the project, leaving Rob to complete the project on his own!

When completed, they were shown on national television and proved to be a great blessing. The series was excellent despite Rob only having limited resources to complete the job. In one scene John Dunn (one of our ministers) was dressed up in a sheet, supposedly representing the Lord Jesus Christ, disappearing in a cloud. The cloud was provided by smoke from a fire that had been lit nearby. The entire series was broadcast on the English Service of ZBC and proved to be very successful for which we praised God.

It was the day after the series was completed that Rob accompanied me to what is now known as The City Sports Centre in Harare. It was there that we were due to have the first Conference of The Pentecostal Fellowship of Zimbabwe. When we had a look around the Sports Centre and saw how cold and uninviting it looked Rob asked what was being done to make it more attractive? When I said that we had not made any plans, he took over. On the day the conference began, we had a large banner on the wall where the speakers would be standing, and huge pot plants decorating the platform. We all agreed that Rob had made a wonderful difference to the venue by what he had accomplished.

But getting back to McChlery, one day I was approached by George King, one of the Elders who had originally moved to the fellowship from The Grange Assembly. He said, **"AB, you really need to make a choice! You cannot continue to do all that you are doing. You need to choose between McChlery or the National Work."**

There was no doubt about it, George was absolutely correct as my involvement in so many different things must have been unhelpful to my local Assembly. As a result, rightly or wrongly, I replied, **"If that is the case, I must concentrate on the National Work."**

As a result, in consultation with the Elders and John Bond it was arranged that I would leave McChlery and it was proposed that Noel Cromhout would come up from South Africa to take my place. My plan was to move to the Midlands so that I was equidistant from Bulawayo and Harare. We had a farewell service and we even received a 'gift' from the Assembly but, everything was about to change, we never left at that time, and Noel never came up to Zimbabwe.

C) MINISTER WITHOUT PORTFOLIO. JULY 1986 – DECEMBER 1988

Sadly, the rest of my story relates largely to how my 'dream' at the 1985 National Conference in Gweru played out in Zimbabwe. It is a sad story and shows that we as Christians are far from perfect and make many mistakes. We are often required to deal with difficult situations in 'church life' no matter what 'church' fellowship we are part of, or what 'Christian' organisation we represent. There will always be problems to overcome, no matter who we are, or where we fellowship. The key is to keep our eyes on the Lord

Jesus, be willing to forgive, and recognise that it is Jesus who 'builds the church,' not us.

No matter how many mistakes we make we can have confidence in what the Lord Jesus stated,

"------I will build My church, and the gates of Hades shall not prevail against it."
Matthew 16.18

So, no matter how often we fail in the end the LORD will not fail! Hallelujah!

Nevertheless, the question has to be,

"Can two walk together, unless they are agreed?"
Amos 3.3

THE NYANGA CONFERENCE 1986

Everything began to change after the meeting in Nyanga which I arranged early in 1986 for our Ministers and Elders. As I prepared for the meeting, my goal was to inspire all of our ministers to seize the challenge of Zimbabwe. I believed strongly that we had to stop closing Assemblies and instead make it our goal to open English Language Assemblies in ALL of the towns right across the country. We knew that all Zimbabweans were learning English at school and so we should believe God to reach out to the whole nation in the English language. Our guest speaker on this occasion was Noel Cromhout who was much loved and respected in all of our fellowships.

His ministry was a great inspiration as always but, there can be no doubt that what transpired was to some degree the result of a challenge that he presented to the entire gathering. It was at the conclusion of one of the meetings that he said something like the following, **"I believe that it is vital that you make a decision as to how you will work with South Africa, now, and in the future!"**

I am sure that he said more than that, but whatever he said, it seemed to me to be a challenge that I could not ignore. As a result, I opened up the meeting to discuss what we should do in respect of our relationship with South Africa. I for one made mention of the fact that during the time I had led the work under John Bond, no minister from South Africa had been made available to fill the gaps left by departing members of our fellowship. This was Despite the fact that most of these departing ministers ended up ministering South of the border! As a result, I was required to find replacement ministers at the rate of 4 new men a year or else close down our Assemblies. As we all knew, this was from a fellowship which at its greatest had numbered only around 20 English Language Assemblies. Sadly, looking back upon it, I do not remember giving credit to the many, like Steve Bacon, who had assisted me in this respect, as many of our new ministers had been recommended to me by others.

As I look back upon what took place at that meeting I am sure that the previous meeting with Brother's Benghu and Bond at McChlery, had a lot to do with the outcome. The demands that had been put upon us had not been forgotten. They had affected the work in Mutare, and resulted in the closure of the Shona work at McChlery. After a lot of conversation, it was decided unanimously, that the time had come to withdraw our churches, from the leadership that John Bond had up and till then provided. It must be recorded that I for one highly valued John Bond and it was with regret that we made this decision, as he was without doubt a great man of God.

Sadly, the effect of this discussion resulted in my plan being put on the back burner, and I was never able to speak about planting an English Language Assembly in every town in the country. Once the 'mini conference' was over, I wasted no time in making an appointment to go and see John Bond in South Africa. On this occasion I didn't go on my own, and believe that there were four of us who travelled together. When we arrived at the meeting we were met by John Bond, Noel Cromhout, John Stegmann, and Neil Gibbs who were all very familiar with the work in Zimbabwe. After presenting the unanimous decision that was taken at the meeting in Nyanga, brother Bond requested that we call another meeting for him to address in Harare. Rightly or wrongly, I felt that it was a fruitless exercise, as the meeting had been unanimous, and so I declined to arrange another meeting. Over the years I often wondered whether I was correct, yet, the last meeting that he and Brother Benghu attended had really brought us to the current situation.

Sadly, our decision to sever 'control' by South Africa, but not 'fellowship,' was misinterpreted and my relationship with John Bond was never the same. As can be imagined, the move of Noel Cromhout from South Africa was now off the table and so although I had had my farewell service I never left. The question was, who was available to move to McChlery as what George King had said was still very valid?

After discussing the situation with the Elders, it was felt that John Baker would be the right person to replace me at McChlery. As a result, John and Sheila Baker moved to Harare in July 1986 allowing me to concentrate on the National work. But having decided that it would not be a good idea to move to the Midlands, I made it clear that we would be remaining in the house in Highlands for the sake of our children's education.

As we would be living in the manse this meant that John and Sheila would need somewhere to live. Since Paul and Cindy Croft had departed for England in October 1985, Philip Chigome was now the minister in Hatfield. As he owned his own house in Hatfield, the 'manse' was not needed, so John and Sheila moved into the Hatfield manse.

Due to the good relationship that we had developed with the Pentecostal Assemblies of Canada the position in Kwe Kwe was filled by Len and Juanita Marrillier who were on loan to us. Len and Juanita were South Africans and Len had a wonderful evangelistic ministry and it was great to have him assisting us.

One of those who travelled to South Africa with me to speak to John Bond was John Dunn. He was a single man who had made a lot of money as a 'chicken farmer' but had sold out some years before. I am not sure when he became a Christian but I know that he had a lot of input into Resthaven, and it was due to his intervention that we had acquired a temporary home there when we first moved to Harare. John had become one of our ministers and was pioneering a work in Borrowdale in his 'garage' which he had converted into a meeting hall. In addition, he was assisting the Lord's work around the country in many ways.

He was a really good man to have around, as he had a heart for the work of God, and his counsel was really valued. Sadly, he died in hospital shortly after becoming ill, and because he had failed to make a last will and testament all his assets were acquired by his family. The Borrowdale Assembly came to an end when his house was sold and the practical assistance that he was providing ceased. I really missed John and when I see him in the presence of the Lord I may well say, **"John, why did you leave us when we needed your counsel and support so much?"**

I know that I am alive as I type these words and if you are reading them, it proves conclusively that you are also alive! But one day we must all die! When John died, he had failed to do some very practical things, like making a 'will.' But he had succeeded in doing the most important thing and that was getting right with God. You may have made a 'will,' you may well have set your earthly house in order but what happens when you die? Have you sorted out where you will go when you die? Do not believe the lies that some people proclaim that it is all over when you die! The Lord Jesus suffered a terrible death to keep you from 'Hell,' do not let His death be in vain! Believe the Good News before it is too late. Turn from your sin, ask Jesus to save you and trust in His death for your eternal salvation. Remember, He did not stay dead, He triumphed over the grave and is alive forever more.

Praise His name!

NATIONAL EXECUTIVE ISSUES.

Although we had withdrawn from South African leadership, we were still part of the Zimbabwe Conference and I was still National Secretary. So, although we were now free to chart our own course as 'English Language Assemblies,' the rest of the Conference still looked to South Africa for leadership. This was not going to be easy and looking back on it, I must confess, that what happened next was inevitable.

A conference was called to take place in 1987, but for some reason the date had been changed. As a result, one of the men representing 'the office,' in Harare implied that there was some ulterior motive behind the change of date. The Chairman Geoffrey Mkwanazi was given a hard time and the atmosphere was not at all pleasant. Having seen how they were treating my friend Geoffrey; I rose to my feet and took the blame for changing the date of the Conference. However, having done that I continued by saying something like the following, **"If this is how we are going to continue then we must sadly withdraw from the fellowship. You can choose to call yourselves by another name, or we will choose another name, but we cannot be part of such a fellowship any longer."**

The response was immediate when one of the men from 'the office' said, **"YOU will need to choose another name as we are the Assemblies of God in Zimbabwe!"**

You may feel that I was far too hasty in making such a decision, however, this was not an isolated incident. At one of the previous conferences some of the 'brethren' were referring to one another as 'coMrade' and there was a lot more that was far from satisfactory. The work that Brother Benghu had established in Zimbabwe had become deeply divided, and sadly after we withdrew, it was years before they were able to call another conference. In fact, the last time that I saw Geoffrey, sometime in the '90s, when visiting from the UK, they had only just managed to have another conference. He told me that over the years he had often considered inviting me back to Zimbabwe, to see if I would be able to assist in calling the brethren together for another conference. I was deeply touched by what he had to say.

As you can see we had now withdrawn from our South African leadership and also from the rest of the work in Zimbabwe. We were now a group of English language Assemblies covering much of the country who were no longer restricted from reaching out to the whole of Zimbabwe as God enabled us.

THE SECOND NYANGA CONFERENCE.

In Tim King's book 'IN SEARCH OF OPHIR' he implies that the following took place at the meeting held early in 1986, however, I am of the opinion that we had two or more meetings in Nyanga and this took place at the following conference.

Having called for this meeting, I was determined that we would move ahead with our Mission to win people to Christ and plant churches in every town in the country. With this in mind, I went to see Steve Bacon to encourage him to share his vision for the country at this gathering. Not only did I ask him to share his vision, but I also told him that I was willing to share the leadership of the work with him and if at a later time the brethren wanted him to take over completely, I would willingly step down.

"THE NYANGA CONFERENCE 1986 (1987?)"

Referring once again to Tim King's book, he records that Steve was the leader of a significant church which met in the centre of Harare called The Christian Life Centre. It had a congregation of 700-800 people and was without doubt, by far the largest multi-racial congregation led by one of our ministers. In fact, it is doubtful that the rest of the movement all around the country could equal the numbers that attended that single church.

Because I was anxious to bring all our churches together, I asked Steve to be the first speaker at this important gathering. However, when the time came, he declined to address the meeting as he felt that what he had to say would not be received sympathetically. The following morning one of the ministers informed me that unless I did something, certain people were going to leave the fellowship. To be quite honest I was amazed as I really did not know what else I could do.

Now I am sure that I could have handled the situation better, and I do regret the actions that I took that day. Nevertheless, when everyone was seated, I addressed the gathering, and explained my dilemma and then said, **"I feel that it is time for us to make a decision, you either want to be part of the work that I am leading or you don't. We cannot continue like this, so please make up your mind today, one way or the other, and while you are making up your mind, I am going to have a little walk."**

Having, clearly presented an option to the meeting, it turned out to be a defining moment for our work in Zimbabwe and by the time the dust had settled, quite a few of the Assemblies had resigned. According to our constitution any Assembly leaving the fellowship needed to call a meeting and put it to the vote with a member of the Executive present. This resulted in me being invited to attend a number of meetings over the next few weeks. One of them was in Triangle where Jannie Nel was ministering. He had come to the Lord under Steve Bacon's ministry and was running a lovely fellowship in the town. It was a sad occasion and only my second visit to the Assembly. I was treated very well by the people but as I had no real link to the Assembly the decision was not difficult to predict.

Another Assembly that decided to withdraw

was Mutare, an Assembly where we had enjoyed living and where we had many happy memories. A lady who I had led to the Lord in Chipinge told me that they **had** to leave the group of churches that I was leading, siting what had taken place when brother's Benghu and Bond had caused us to close the Shona works that we were operating. I could understand if that were the current situation, but of course that problem had long since been resolved and should not have been presented as a reason to withdraw.

After the meeting in Mutare something amazing took place on my way home. As I drove down the road, I knew that I ought to be broken-hearted! The Mutare Assembly, where I had laboured so hard, amongst others, had voted to reject MY LEADERSHIP and leave the group of churches that I was leading. However, instead of being heartbroken, I spent the time driving back to Harare praising God. In fact, my heart was bursting with joy and I really couldn't understand why? My head told me that I ought to be very upset but my heart was praising God!

When I travelled down to Kwe Kwe to attend their meeting, I was very aware that the situation was complex. The Pentecostal Assemblies of Canada had made it clear that they were unwilling to loan Len Marrilliar to the Kwe Kwe Assembly indefinitely. In fact, they had made it clear that he could only stay if the work came under their oversight. Len and his wife were very popular with the members of the Assembly and at that point we definitely did not have a replacement for him. However, when the vote was taken it was 50-50 and therefore, had I insisted, the

Assembly would have continued under my leadership.

Nevertheless, knowing that we could not provide a new Minister at that time, I suggested that they have one more vote, and this time the vote was in favour of leaving. Some may question my actions, as there were valuable assets involved. As an example, we had a valuable church building and a lovely manse, assets that had been paid for over the years by dedicated members of the assembly. Nevertheless, had I insisted, we may well have ended up with a manse and church building and no congregation. So, the decision that I took that day must be left in the hands of the Lord!

Praise God, the work that I had a hand in establishing has continued. Sometime later I was advised by one of the Canadian missionaries that the church in Kwe Kwe was flourishing. He knew that I had been instrumental in establishing the church and felt that I would be encouraged by the news. Naturally I was able to praise God when I heard what he had to say!

Another Assembly that withdrew at this time was Bethshan in Bulawayo. Nevertheless, the current leadership were unwilling for me to attend the meeting, and voted to leave the fellowship in the absence of any Executive member being present.

I am not proud of what took place, I am deeply saddened. Perhaps it was mainly as a result of the huge changes that were taking place in our country, for example the continuing departure of key personnel. Whatever the reason it is possible that we could have achieved so much more had we been willing to pull together.

Shortly after these events I met one of the ministers at the Post Office in Highlands and he said something like the following, **"I am amazed that nothing has been done to heal the breach!"**

As he walked away, I was puzzled and wanted to ask him, what more could I have done?

Anyway, one evening, having just returned from a meeting in Beatrice, I picked up a book to read in the bath before going to bed. The book that I chose to read that evening was called **"A WORD TO THE WISE"** by **Donald Gee**. It had been given to me by John Bond some time before when I was at a conference in South Africa. I must admit that when he gave me the book I was impressed, feeling quite sure that Brother Bond knew what he was doing! But it was only later, that I realised, that he was wanting me to **'get wise!'** He had not been thinking that **I was particularly wise** when he had given me the book!

However, while reading this book in the bath, the Lord suddenly spoke to me very clearly from the following Proverb,

"Where there is no counsel, the people fall; but in the multitude of counsellors there is safety." **Proverbs 11.14**

I am not too sure why this verse spoke to my heart in the way it did, but it was as if the Lord had walked into the room and spoken directly to me. He made it clear that I had to apologise for the part that I had played in what had taken place! Not only that, but in doing so, I was not to try and excuse myself in any way at all! The only thing that I was to do was to apologise! I was not to try and explain my actions, or try to blame anyone else, I was only required to apologise for my part in what had taken place!

Having heard so clearly from the Lord, I set about doing what He had shown me. I was able to visit certain of the brethren in person, but sadly others I could only contact by phone, and still others I could only contact by mail. Among the brethren I definitely wrote to was Steve Bacon, and I spoke personally to John Potter. I even spoke to Martin Emmerson, who had not been at the meeting in Nyanga, and as far as I am aware I contacted everyone that I needed to speak to, in order to apologise for what had taken place. It was not an easy thing to do, as I was not able to defend myself in any way, but I know that it was what God required.

It was not long after all of this had taken place, that I had a phone call from Geoff Gonifas who was now living in England. He said something like the following, **"Hi AB, Geoff here, how are you doing? We are considering returning from the UK to Zimbabwe and I would like to work with you if you will have me?"**

After all that had been taking place, to receive a call like that was almost overwhelming. I was deeply moved by Geoff's call and was so choked up that I found it difficult to speak. We had just experienced a major split in the work and here was my friend Geoff volunteering to return to Zimbabwe and work with me again. I will never forget his call as it was such an encouragement to me! Thank you, Geoff!!

Naturally, I explained what had taken place to Geoff on the phone, but despite that he did come out for a visit. Yet, instead of returning to Zimbabwe, not long afterwards, an opportunity opened up in the USA, and they left the UK and have been in America ever since. Despite that, his phone call and visit were a great blessing to Mally and myself!

THE NEW COVENANT ASSEMBLIES OF GOD.

As a result of all that had taken place, we needed to reorganise ourselves. Among other things we needed a name, as we could not all have the same name. After a lot of discussion Stu Macdonald came up with a name and as a result, the 'New Covenant Assemblies of God' came into being in March 1987.

But because we had not given up on the idea of a closer involvement with the Canadians, our new constitution was largely modelled upon their constitution, both for the local church and the movement. This resulted in a few problems which I will not go into now and at one stage while we were discussing the new constitution, I foolishly said something like the following, **"If we fail to agree, then I will have to resign!"**

I was in the wrong and my good friend Malcolm Fraser described my attitude very well when he said, **"You behaved like a little Hitler!"**

Although that was very hard to take, in many ways Malcolm was perfectly correct. It is good to have friends who are not afraid to put you in your place!

But despite my behaviour the New Covenant Assemblies of God came into existence. At its inception it included the following Assemblies: McChlery, Marondera- (English and a Shona work) Hatfield – (English and a Shona work) Gweru, Kadoma, Redcliff,

Shurugwe, and Chitungwiza which was a Shona work. In addition, we had outreaches in Beatrice and elsewhere and not long afterwards we also established a new Assembly in Bulawayo.

The following were duly elected to the National Executive: Stuart MacDonald, Simon Rhodes, and yours truly as Chairman.

P.O. BOX FM 154
FAMONA
BULAWAYO
ZIMBABWE

A. B. ROBERTSON (MINISTER)
NATIONAL CHAIRMAN

TELEPHONE OFFICE (19) 65302   HOME (19)45080

The National Chairman's
Card

THE NEW COVENANT ASSEMBLIES OF GOD
FOUNDATION MEMBER'S
CERTIFICATE OF ORDINATION

This is to certify that

JOHN EDWARD TERRY BAKER

having given evidence of his divine gift and calling to the Ministry of the Gospel of Christ and having consecrated himself to that calling, according to the word of God, and having met the requirements prescribed by

THE NEW COVENANT ASSEMBLIES OF GOD

has on this TWENTY THIRD day of JANUARY 19 88

by the laying on of hands and the prayers of the National Executive of the New Covenant Assemblies of God, been set apart and Ordained to the Ministry of the Gospel.

The National Executive of the New Covenant Assemblies of God, hereby recognises his Divine Calling and Ordination and confers on him the right to

PREACH THE WORD

and exercise all functions pertaining to the Christian Ministry, so long as he remains in fellowship with the New Covenant Assemblies of God and his spirit and practice are such as become the Gospel of Christ.

We acknowledge this day FOUR years of unbroken service to the Assemblies of God as a Minister of the Gospel having first received the laying on of hands for the ministry in the year 1983.

In witness whereof, the duly authorised officers of

The New Covenant Assemblies of God

have set their hand

This TWENTY THIRD day of JANUARY 19 88

_____ National Chairman
_____ National Secretary

Valid only when accompanied by the Annual Ministerial Credential of the New Covenant Assemblies of God.

"Go ye therefore, and teach all nations, baptising them in the name of the Father, and the Son and of the Holy Ghost: teaching them to observe all things whatsoever I have commanded you: and lo, I am with you always, even unto the end of the world" — Matt. 28: 19 & 20.

NCAOG FOUNDATION MEMBERS CERTIFICATE OF ORDINATION. PHOTO NUMBER 25 THE NATIONAL CHAIRMAN

As I was no longer the senior minister at McChlery Avenue I was no longer entitled to an office at the church. As a result, the NCAOG head office was moved to our outside spare bedroom. When we compared ourselves to the Head Office of the PAOC in Toronto which was huge and so very impressive we were so small and insignificant. In fact, one of the reasons that we never linked up with the Canadians was that we were so small! We felt that we would be just swallowed up, if we joined such a large organisation.

As a result of the confusion that had taken place about my leaving McChlery Avenue and going to the Midlands, my very good secretary had found a new job and was no longer available. But the Lord was good and a young man named Gary Reeves became my office assistant. He was a great help despite not having the experience of Marietta Beale.

But we had a problem as John Baker was not at all happy living in Hatfield as it was some miles from the Assembly where he was ministering. As a result, when he found a suitable property just down the road from the Assembly he wanted to move. This naturally put me in a bit of a spot as I was occupying the manse and money was urgently needed to purchase the new house. After some consideration a medium-term solution was found which involved selling the house in Chipinge where we no longer had an Assembly. This would enable us to purchase the Highlands house in the name of the 'National Development Fund,' enabling us to continue to live in Highlands and enabling John and Sheila to move to Eastlea.

The money was needed urgently and the sale of the

house in Chipinge would take time. When I shared the problem with one of my long-term friends he offered to lend me the money until the house was sold so that the transaction could take place. I praise God for men who are willing, and able, to help the work of God financially. Initially I was going to mention his name but on second thoughts I decided not to. He was always a great blessing to me personally and I honour him for his faithfulness to the Lord! As soon as the house was sold the money was paid back.

THE NEW BULAWAYO ASSEMBLY.

As previously mentioned, Bethshan Tabernacle in Bulawayo had withdrawn from the group of churches that I was leading. Sadly, during the months that followed many of the congregation left Bethshan and the congregation became a great deal smaller than it had been before. Some had left the country, as was the case with all our congregations, but many had left to seek fellowship in other churches around the town. However, I was unaware of what was happening in Bulawayo until I received a call from someone advising me of the situation. I was informed that the congregation had dwindled from around 200 when Gary Smith was the minister, to around 30 people, and even some of those were considering leaving. When I heard who those remaining people were, and that they were now planning to leave, I felt that I needed to take action. I knew that they were really faithful men and woman who would not be leaving unless something was very wrong.

As a result, I phoned Craig Friend who was now

in secular business in Bulawayo and asked him to arrange a meeting of interested people. I only informed Craig and one other person that I was coming to Bulawayo but on the evening in question 24 people attended the meeting held in a room in a local hotel. As it happened all of those who were present were known by myself.

After opening the meeting in prayer, I spent the first five minutes or so putting the people in the picture. Things had changed dramatically in the 'movement' since I had last been in Bulawayo. As a result, I felt that it was vital that they were aware of our changed circumstances before we started. But before I finished, I was interrupted when someone called out, **"AB, all we want to know is whether you can do something for us or not? If not, we can all go home, but if you can, we would like to know, so that we can consider it before making any decision."**

Having been put on the spot I made the following reply, **"I am about to go on holiday and so I cannot do anything until I return. However, starting at the beginning of February next year, if you can find a suitable venue, I will provide you with a regular Sunday morning meeting. If it is available, the venue that we are currently meeting in today could meet our needs initially. I will be here for the first meeting, and from then on, the meetings will be conducted by myself or fellow ministers from around the country. As and when required we will add a Sunday evening meeting, Bible studies and so on. That is all that I am willing to offer you this evening and if you are interested, please give me your name, address and telephone number before you leave!"**

As there was little more to be said, having closed

in prayer, the meeting came to an end.

After our usual Christmas holiday to visit to my mother in Cape Town, true to my word, I was back in Bulawayo early in 1987. It is interesting to note that at the very first meeting of the new Assembly the same number of people attended as had attended the exploratory meeting but not exactly the same people. Praise God, the work proved to be a great success right from the beginning. Every week one of our ministers from around the country travelled down to Bulawayo to take the Sunday meeting. I was really encouraged by their willingness to support the work in Bulawayo and it was not long before other weekly meetings were added. In addition, as a result of the increased numbers attending the meetings, it was not long before it was necessary to find a bigger venue.

Before saying anything more about Bulawayo, I must mention Masvingo. For some years we had an Assembly in Masvingo, but it had closed down before I took over from Neil Gibbs. Anyhow, for some reason I visited the town and met up with Billy and Glenda Nel whom we had last seen some years before in Mutare. I am not sure how it all took place, but Billy became one of our 'visiting preachers' in our new fellowship in Bulawayo. He was, at the time, in fellowship with the Full Gospel Church in Masvingo but travelled to Bulawayo fairly frequently. It was really amazing how the Lord provided for this new fellowship in Bulawayo!

TEN WEEKS SABBATICAL LEAVE IN THE UK.

With everything that had been taking place, the last few years had been very demanding. As a result, someone, I am not sure who, suggested that what I needed to do was to take a Sabbatical. Although the idea was attractive to me, where would we go, and how would we pay for the whole trip? As I meditated on the idea, a plan formed in my mind and one day I suggested to Mally that we ought to go on a 'sabbatical' to the UK as soon as possible.

I planned to sell the car in order to raise the money for our return tickets to England. We would trust God to meet our transport needs when we returned. Then, amongst other things, we would contact my aunt Diana who lived just outside London in Twickenham, and ask her if we could base ourselves with her. We would then contact my friend Ray Belfield in Wigan in the North of England and see if he could arrange some preaching engagements for me. Having done these things, we would then look to God and see how it all came together.

Having made these preliminary plans, I was sure that the Lord was leading us, when we were offered accommodation for at least eight of the ten weeks that we would be away. Ray was able to arrange accommodation in the home of a family that he knew for six of those weeks. The family would be away all Summer at a youth camp and were willing to make their home available to us. My aunt agreed to have us stay at her home for a couple of weeks or more. In addition, Ray arranged ministry opportunities for me every Sunday that we would be in England, and Nelson Hogg provided us with a car for the entire period we were in the UK for £50.00 a week.

Having had such a wonderful response from England, we decided to go ahead with our plans. As a result, we sold the car, booked and paid for the flights, and were all set to go when things began to go wrong. It all started when we had a letter from my aunt who said,

Dear Alan,

Sadly, I will have to withdraw my offer of accommodation for you and the family when you come to England. I have been a spinster all my life and I do not think I could entertain three young boys for more than a few days. Anything more would be too much."

Love Diana

I am sure that she said a little more than that but for us, that was the relevant part. It was a big blow as you can imagine, but worse was to follow. I had hardly finished reading the letter when I had a phone call from Ray who said, **"Abe,** (He always called me Abe) **I am so sorry to inform you that the offer of accommodation that I told you about has been withdrawn. When the couple offered you their home, they had forgotten that they had arranged for builders to do some renovations whilst they were away. I am so sorry, but you will not be able to stay at their home this summer. They have asked me to apologise on their behalf as they are very sorry to let you down."**

Having received this news, what could we do, it was too late to change our plans! The car had been sold, and the flights were all paid for. Not only that but Paddy and Astrid Gobbett (another Minister) would be staying in our house whilst we were away. So, despite our accommodation plans having collapsed, we were going, and would have to trust the Lord to open a way for us. I made one more call, this time to Geoff and Diana Gonifas in Northampton in England. It was Diana who answered the phone and our conversation went something like this, **"Good morning, Diana,"** I said, **"It's AB here, I trust that you are all well? We have a slight problem! We are leaving for England in a couple of days on 'sabbatical' leave, that is Mally, Mark, Matthew, Jonathan and myself. We are planning to be in the UK for ten weeks. Up and till today we had at least eight weeks accommodation arranged out of the ten weeks that we will be in England. Sadly, things have changed and we now only have accommodation arranged for a few days. I am sorry to have to ask, but would you and Geoff be willing to give us a bed for a few days?"**

She replied, **"Hi AB, Lovely to hear from you. That will be no problem at all. We would love to have you, Mally, and the boys and look forward to seeing you all again."**

Having now been guaranteed a couple of nights' accommodation in two different homes there was nothing more that I could do except put our trip into the hands of the Lord. Was it not He who met our needs when we went to Israel some time before? I did not know how, but I knew that God would not let us down as we set out to spend ten weeks in the United Kingdom!

Despite my confidence, there was another problem. Once again, almost all of our yearly 'foreign currency allowance' had already been used in a previous trip to South Africa. As a result, when the five of us boarded the plane to take us to the UK for ten weeks, we were only allowed something like £100.00 in

British currency. Naturally this did not look very good as our 'hire' car alone would be costing us £500.00!

As our son, Mark, was more aware of what was happening than the other boys, he turned to me as we were about to fly out of Harare and said, **"Dad, we are mad to be travelling to England with so little money!"**

However, the ten weeks that we spent in the UK were truly a miracle of God's provision but as it is a long story, I will not be telling it now. But, having whet your appetite I will share a few of the things that took place during those ten eventful weeks.

Once we had picked up the car at the airport, as originally planned we headed for my aunt Diana's home in Twickenham. She was very hospitable as usual and soon warmed to our 'well-behaved' sons which proved to be a real blessing to us all. In fact, I believe that she fell in love with our sons and when she died some years later, she specifically set aside some money for each of them in her will.

Surprisingly, when we arrived at her home, there was some mail waiting for us. There was a letter from another aunt, my mother's sister, Beryl. When I opened the envelope, I was pleasantly surprised to find a short note from my aunt explaining that the enclosed cheque for £500.00, was a belated wedding present for Mally and myself. If that was not enough whilst we were there, we received a letter from a couple who were attending our meetings in Beatrice. They were on holiday in Europe and when they heard that we were going on a sabbatical, they decided to give us a 'tithe' of their 'foreign currency' which turned out to be around £150.00.

I believe that those two gifts were a wonderful

confirmation that God would not let us down and that He would provide for us the whole time that we were away. Yet another miracle took place which actually began when John Baker took us to the airport in Harare. I am sure that he did not know the real state of my finances when he said, **"AB I want to give you my mother's address and phone number in England. If you run out of money, my mother has access to my savings and she will be able to help you. Please make use of it if you need to do so."**

We thanked John for his generosity, and thoughtfulness, but I was adamant that we would not use his funds unless it was a real emergency, and then we would return the money just as soon as we were able. It is hard to believe what happened later whilst we were in England, but even though we do not always plan ahead I praise God that He does!

It was around midway through our visit to England that we spent a wonderful weekend with some relatives. However, when we left their home early on the Monday morning we were out of cash and not sure what to do next. It was then that I realised that we were actually in the same town where John's mother lived. As a result, it was early that Monday morning that I phoned Mrs. Baker and asked if we could come around and visit, explaining that we were friends of John's.

When we arrived at her home, despite the fact that she was in the middle of her weekly wash she was delighted to see us and made us very welcome. We enjoyed a pot of tea with her and John's sister, who were anxious to hear all the news about John and Sheila. After a decent interval I explained the reason for our visit and Mrs. Baker went immediately to draw out some money for us from John's account. God had provided for us once again and sometime later we were on our way.

As I was determined to return the money to John before we left for home, I only asked for £100.00 but, within 24 hours I realised my mistake. I ought to have borrowed at least £200.00 as after filling up with petrol, enjoying an evening meal, and paying for bed and breakfast accommodation for the five of us, the following day we were once again out of cash.

We spent part of the next day in a park in the Cotswolds, unsuccessfully trying to fly a kite. We then found ourselves in Stroud where I spent a considerable amount of time in a telephone box making calls. We had accommodation arranged for Saturday and Sunday as I would be preaching in Phil and Ursula Hamilton's Elim fellowship that Sunday, but the next few days were a problem. Phil and Ursula were originally members of our Mutare Assembly and were lovely people with two sons older than ours.

We enjoyed a lovely weekend with them although it was quite a squeeze as it was only a small flat. The boys were all crammed into one bedroom with bunk-beds. Sadly, our youngest son, Jonathan, had very smelly shoes. They were new shoes which we had purchased in England but despite being 'new' they had become very smelly. The next morning, we discovered that his shoes had been thrown out of the window by one of the older boys never to be found again. He had been unable to take the smell and having found the guilty objects he had tossed them out of the window. As they were the only shoes that Jonathan had with him, he had to walk 'barefoot' to the shop to get a new pair that morning.

Meanwhile, back in Stroud I was having a problem as no one was answering my calls. It was summer and a lot of people were no doubt away on holiday, or else they knew that it was me phoning!! One of the numbers I tried time and time again but somehow, I was unable to get through. It was only late in the day that I discovered that I was missing out one digit when phoning. When I dialled the correct number, I got through immediately but, I must backtrack a little before we continue.

You will remember that I had phoned Geoff and Diana Gonifas and they agreed to have us for a couple of nights. Those couple of nights turned out to be much more and they were incredibly good to us during our stay in England.

One day whilst we were with them we went to the shopping centre. A local church could be accessed from this new indoor shopping centre and we discovered that John Knight was their senior minister. If you remember he was the Anglican minister who had come to know the Lord some years before in Mutare. They had literally been forced to flee Zimbabwe and after much difficulty he had eventually been appointed to this position in Northampton. I had been told about John by Geoff but we were all amazed when we happened to bump into him in the shopping centre. It took place when we were searching for Jonathan, who had gone missing for a few minutes. Our conversation had been very short but went something like this, **"My word, AB and Mally, what are you doing here?"** John asked.

"Hi John, Good to see you!" I replied, "Geoff told us that you were now in Northampton, we are having a sabbatical and have come to spend a total of 10 weeks in the UK."

"My it is so good to see you all," he said, "but sadly, I have got to go, but please do not leave Northampton without coming to see us, as we would love to see you all.".

During our short conversation John provided us with his card but sadly we had not been able to get to see them before we left town. It was John that I had been trying unsuccessfully to phone. We had something to eat just before I went once more to the phone booth, this time with the correct number. We went to a nearby supermarket and bought some food, and then sat down at a park bench to eat our meal. Before we gave thanks I said, **"This is the 'last supper' and I do not know where we will spend the night tonight. After we have eaten, I am going to make one more phone call."**

Maybe I ought not to have said that, however, God had not forgotten us and when I phoned the correct number, the phone was answered immediately,

-

"John Knight here, can I help you?"

"Hi John, AB here. My apologies for not contacting you sooner. We are presently in Stroud in the Cotswolds and we are in a bit of trouble. We have a full tank of petrol but we have nowhere to stay tonight. We have accommodation where I am preaching this coming weekend but we have nowhere to stay until then. There is some cash in the pipeline but it is not available yet. Could you put us up for a couple of nights?"

"No problem," he said, "We would love to have you. For the last year, since having to flee Zimbabwe, we have been living in other people's houses. Finally, we have our own home and it has everything that switches on and off. We have plenty of room and would be thrilled to put you up."

Having received directions from John, I went to share the good news with the family and we were soon on our way. Our God had once again gone ahead of us. Praise His name!

Our stay with John and Jill was a real blessing to all of us. They could not have been kinder and we were made to feel very much at home. Since leaving Zimbabwe, they had been through an awful lot. Due to political pressure the Anglican Church leaders in Zimbabwe refused to give John a reference. As a result, he had been unable to get a position in England and they had been living in 'other people's houses' for an entire year. It was only as a result of the intervention of the retired Archbishop of Harare that he finally obtained a position. As a result, they were more than willing to share their new home with 'homeless' Zimbabweans.

Whilst we were there, I was able to read a book that John had written called 'RAIN IN A DRY LAND' which had been printed the year before. It was an inspiring read and is still available. There is no doubt that our stay with the Knight's had been arranged by the Lord and we were so very thankful for the wonderful blessing they were to us.

We also stayed with Paul and Cindy Croft during our time in England, but I cannot remember preaching at the Assembly on that occasion. They had moved from Hatfield in Zimbabwe, to Cleveleys near Blackpool, and were trying to resurrect an Assembly that had all but closed down. When we visited them, they were living in a one-bedroomed flat over some shops in the middle of Cleveleys. As a result, when the Robertson's came to stay it was wall to wall people. They were very gracious to have us and it was a joy to see them again. Sometime before they left for England, I had the joy of officiating at their wedding in Hatfield.

During our sabbatical, we had many adventures including a visit to Scotland where we stayed with another ex-Zimbabwean Pastor and his wife and I was privileged to preach in the Paisley Assembly. Whilst staying with Ben and Brenda Pitout, we took the opportunity to drive up to Loch Lomond and then up as far as Oban. The day was dull, drizzly and cold but as we drove into Oban we drove into brilliant sunshine. We spent a half hour or so exploring a ruined castle and then because it was getting rather late, we made our way back to Paisley. By the time we arrived back at their home, our hosts were beginning to get a little worried about what had happened to the Robertson's.

Our sabbatical finally came to an end and it was time to head back home. It had been an amazing experience and the Lord had watched over us all of the way. The people we stayed with were extremely kind, and except for the one episode where one of the sons of our gracious hosts threw the 'extremely smelly' shoes of our son, Jonathan, out of the window, never to be found again, we were treated with great consideration and love.

Our flight home was a blessing, we arrived at

the airport on the correct day, and we were met at Harare airport by John Baker and put in the picture as regards developments while we had been away. It was good to be home!

TRANSPORT PROBLEMS.

I cannot remember the exact order of events but transport became a major problem when we returned to Zimbabwe. A few years before, we had possessed two Nissan Pulsar motor cars. One belonged to the 'work' which I used to travel around the country and the other was our own. Somewhere along the line I sold the car belonging to the 'work' as we needed the money in the National Development Fund. I felt that it was not right for us to have two cars if we could not meet the salaries of all our ministers. The other car had been sold to finance our sabbatical leave in the UK.

Because I had seen the hand of God work in my situation previously, I waited for the Lord to once again come to my aid. He did come to our aid but not in the way that I expected. Prior to that, I walked, was given lifts, borrowed cars and may well have taken taxis on occasion as well.

Our neighbour was Mrs. Winter, the mother of Billy Winter, who preached the message from the book of Amos, which had made such an impression upon me at the South African General Conference in 1969. She was a lovely Christian lady who had served the Lord for many years. In a conversation one day she told me that Ezekiel Gutu, the leader of Zimbabwe Assemblies of God Africa, had held meetings in the garage in her home in Highlands when he first began to preach.

When she realised our situation, she kindly loaned us the use of her car on a number of occasions, which was greatly appreciated.

It was John Baker who came to the rescue when he gave us a Citroen DS motorcar. It was an amazing ride as the suspension was fantastic. Just down the road from our home was a traffic hump, one of the first that we had come upon, which was a real problem for any normal car. With the Citroen it wasn't necessary to slow down, you just seemed to float over the bump. Sadly, some months later my garage informed me that it would cost a great deal to repair the car (nothing to do with the humps) and foolishly we did not proceed. To be quite honest, it was the most comfortable car that I have ever driven and I was grateful to have had the opportunity to own it even if it was only for such a short time.

It was then that Rob Mackenzie came to our rescue with a VW Passat. It proved to be a real blessing and lasted us until we left Zimbabwe, when we gave it to someone else. We were really humbled that fellow ministers were the ones that came to our rescue at that time. Thank you, my brethren.

THE PRIDE OF LIFE.

I nearly left the following incident out of my story but feel that it is just too good to miss. It all began when I was having a serious conversation with Mally. In all seriousness I remember saying, **"There are really only three sins that we need to be careful about and all sin is related to these three. They are, 1) The Lust of the Eyes, 2) The Lust of the Flesh, and 3) The Pride of Life. I know that I need to be careful about the first** two but I feel that I do not need to be too concerned about The Pride of Life!"

I was quite serious but God was about to show me something.

Sometime later we had a ministers meeting and we gathered together in the office belonging to one of our ministers. We had only just arrived and we were greeting one another as we had not been together for some time when the phone rang. Because we were making such a racket the local minister could not hear what his caller was saying as a result in a very loud voice he said, **"Shut up ----- I am on the phone and I cannot hear what is being said!"**

There was an immediate hush as we all stopped speaking. But although I stopped speaking my immediate thoughts were, **"Who does he think he is shouting at us like that? I am in charge of this meeting. How dare he speak to us like that!"**

Despite this we had a great meeting as I was privileged to work with a great group of men. Later on, when I was getting into my borrowed car (Mrs. Winter's) I decided that I would have to speak to the minister about his behaviour when I heard the Lord say quite clearly, **"Do you know why you are upset? It's your PRIDE!"**

I never did speak about this incident again as the Lord had truly put me in my place. Please remember that we all need to be careful about each and every one of these three sins!

NEW ADAMS FARM MASSACRE.

Sadly, in November 1987 another terrible massacre took place in Zimbabwe. The 'war' had been over for seven years and this was the last thing that we expected to take place. One of our ministers, Simon Rhodes, his wife Rina and their son Adam had been part of a Christian Community Farm outside Bulawayo for a short while, but they never really settled and then moved back into full time ministry.

For a short time, they had lived at 'New Adams Farm' which with 'Olive Tree Farm' was run by the Pentecostal Community of Reconciliation. The farms were located at Esigodini which is 65 miles south of Bulawayo. On the night of Wednesday, the 25th November a rebel group came onto the farms and proceeded to murder 16 people, which included two infants and three children. One child was spared by the murderers and another child managed to escape.

One of the founders of the community was John Russell who was now seventy-four years old. He was the principal shareholder in Russell Construction, an earthmoving business in Bulawayo. He was flying home from the USA that Wednesday night when the killers struck. Members of his family had been murdered that night and, as can be expected, he was completely shattered at the news. The funeral in Bulawayo was conducted by Simon Rhodes and was a very sad affair.

A BRITISH VISITOR.

Sometime after our sabbatical in the UK, we had a visit from Gary Stevenson. My good friend Ray Belfield had suggested that Gary would be a blessing to our Assemblies and we were delighted to have him visit. We arranged a meeting for him to speak to all our ministers and other leaders, and he also visited a number of different Assemblies around the country. When we were in Marondera the weather was very cold and wet and Gary complained that he could have stayed in England and enjoyed the same type of weather. I remember saying, **"Gary, do not worry your next appointment is in Bulawayo and it hardly ever rains there. I can assure you that you will enjoy some sunshine in Bulawayo, next weekend!"**

When Gary returned from Bulawayo he said, **"I thought you said it would be sunny in Bulawayo! It rained the whole time that I was there!"**

Praise God for the rain, there was no doubt that it was needed in Bulawayo and I suggested that perhaps it was Gary who had brought the rain. Despite his 'complaints' about the weather, his ministry was a great encouragement and a blessing to us all and we were sad to see him return to the UK!

TEA & SCONES AT BARBOURS.

Sometime during our five years in Harare we learned of a very special event. We were told that a number of local ministers and their wives used to meet for tea and scones at Barbours on a Monday morning. Barbours was THE DEPARTMENT STORE in Harare and they had a restaurant on the roof. Mally and I went a number of times and enjoyed the most delicious scones that you could find anywhere. The TEA was most likely TANGANDA TEA produced near Chipinge, the milk, butter and cream were produced by cows in our incredibly successful dairy industry. This was all put together with delicious strawberry jam.

But despite the attraction of tea and scones at

Barbours, our time in Harare had come to an end, we were on our way back to Bulawayo!

Chapter 3

THE FINAL CHAPTER.

THE RETURN TO BULAWAYO! December 1988

The past five years in Harare had been very full and although we were very happy things had to change for a number of reasons. As I have already mentioned I was no longer being supported by my own congregation. I had chosen to concentrate all my efforts upon the National work. However, the resources in the National Development Fund were limited! I really needed to have the financial support of a local fellowship.

In addition, the work that we had established in Bulawayo just under two years before needed a full-time minister and it was my intention to be that man. Lastly, we had to do something about Mark's education. For a number of reasons, the two schools that he had attended in Harare had proved to be unsatisfactory. There was good 'private schools' in the Harare area but the fees were out of our reach. But, despite the 'fees,' Mark did end up going to a 'private school' in Bulawayo.

Our move back to Bulawayo at the end of 1988 was really traumatic. In fact, it seemed that every time we moved, it just got that much more difficult. There were of course five of us, but ----- we also had 3 dogs, Bruno, Rocky and Heidi and one cat whose name I have forgotten. In addition, it was only after the removals van had gone, that I discovered that a whole lot of things had been left behind. As a result, the car was really packed when we finally set out on our journey.

By the time it was all over I vowed that next time we moved, we would sell the lot and start again at the other end. As it happened that is exactly what took place, and it was less than twelve months later, I might add.

As we were aware that it would be late in the day before the removals van set out from our home, we arranged to spend the night in a lodge in 'Lake McIlwaine Game Park.' Our faithful servant Cosmos stayed overnight at the house in order to look after the cat and dogs. The following day the cat and the dogs were picked up by some friends and taken to the railway station. They then travelled overnight by train to Bulawayo where we picked them up and took them to our new home.

As we were leaving and Cosmos was not coming with us, he desperately needed a new job. Our neighbours, recent arrivals from the UK, were in need of a reliable servant. Despite this job opportunity Cosmos was not interested as he had seen the way they treated their gardener! He told us that he wanted a Christian employer like us. As we were concerned for him, we arranged for him to be employed as a security guard in the firm owned by someone from our congregation but sadly, he did not last long. When I enquired sometime later, I learned that he had fallen asleep on the job and as a result lost his position.

But, getting back to our move, it was already quite late by the time we finished cleaning the house and packing the car. We set out on the short journey to the lake and arrived just before the gates were shut for the night. Our lodge was wonderful and it would have been great to have spent more time there, but we had to leave first thing in the morning. So, after a restful night, we set out for Bulawayo. Some five or so hours later, we arrived safely at our new home after a rather 'squashed' journey, and praised God for journeying mercies.

Our new home was a three bedroomed house at number 8 Milton Avenue, Malindela, Bulawayo. It was not as big as our former home in Highlands and was built upon a plot of land about a quarter of the size. But the house was situated in a lovely quiet neighbourhood on a jacaranda tree lined avenue. In addition, it had a beautiful flamboyant tree just outside the front door and a swimming pool in the front garden, which proved to be a great blessing to all the family.

Our possessions were all safely delivered, and the following morning we set out for the railway station to pick up the rest of the family. As can be expected, the dogs were thrilled to see us, and seemed none the worse for the experience. But sadly, the cat had another story to tell. He had been placed in a cardboard container during the journey and it seemed that he had spent the whole night trying to get out. As a result, the box was badly damaged, and he was absolutely exhausted. When he arrived at his new home he lay down on the floor and did not move for hours.

I had not selected the house, but had left it to Billy and Glenda Nel who were now living in Bulawayo. He had managed to get a transfer on the railways and had resigned from his job, and was now working full time in our new Assembly which was thriving under their care.

It was wonderful to have members of our previous congregation come around and welcome us back 'home,' and each one was a blessing. Among those who came were John and Rose Blackmore who had been faithful members of the new congregation right from the beginning. In fact, they had been among the 24 people at the 'exploratory meeting' where we discussed the establishment of a new assembly. Another person who visited us soon after our arrival was Craig Friend who had been instrumental in arranging that 'exploratory meeting' over two years before. He and his wife Georgie were attending another church in Bulawayo. After a short visit he left, but not before he had pressed a wad of notes into my hand and said, **"AB, I am sure that you are short of cash after your move to Bulawayo and as Christmas is just around the corner, I think you could use this."**

I was overwhelmed by his generosity as he had given me Z$700.00. He had been quite correct about our financial situation and his gift was very welcome. How good is our God and how generous are His people! Praise His wonderful name!

The Assembly was growing and it was lovely to meet up with many of our old friends from Bethshan as well as many new people. As we had no 'church' building in Bulawayo, Billy rented a large office in the centre of town. This open plan office was then converted into three separate rooms. This enabled Billy, myself and my secretary to have a separate office each.

I was very fortunate to have Eleanor Lobb, as my secretary whilst in Bulawayo. She was a lovely girl and one of the daughters of Errol and Davril who I had known from Middle Sabi days.

As there was a music practice every week, I asked if I could come along and try my hand at playing my violin which I had not played for years. I was thrilled to discover that I was still able to play, and after a few practices, the other musicians encouraged me to play with them at the following Sunday morning meeting. I was thrilled at the opportunity, but, was not prepared for what happened next! That Sunday, after we had sung a few songs, Billy who was leading the morning meeting said, **"And now we will have the violin by itself."**

I naturally played, remember the 'Quartet' which became a 'duet' at the South African Conference? Nevertheless, like singing in front of 2000 + people, at the conference at Witbank in South Africa, it was the last time that I was asked to play a violin solo! Despite that, I think most of the congregation returned the following week!

I am not sure when it happened but Billy became the Chaplin of the Christian Motorcycle Association. As a result, on a number of occasions we had a large number of big motorcycles parked outside the hall where we were meeting. Praise God, the new assembly was having a wider impact than we could imagine.

THE FAMILY.

It seems incredible, but I still have a copy of the

Christmas newsletter that I sent out that year which I include below,

8 Milton Avenue,
Malindela,
Bulawayo.
Dear -----------,

As you can see from the above, we have now moved to Bulawayo. It was a hard decision to make after 5+ years in Harare but now that we have moved, I believe it has been the correct decision. This letter is by way of a news update on our family and I trust it will be a blessing to you.

At the beginning of 1988 Mally was told by her doctor that she had a "Mixed Connective Tissue Disorder," which gives her a lot of pain and she only finds relief taking a very strong pain killer. This has been a real problem for Mally which we are really looking to God to heal but because of it 1988 was a very difficult year for her. We trust that 1989 will be a year of healing and blessing.

Mark is now 13 and has completed his first year at high school. Again, a very difficult year! He started at Churchill, but after one term we moved him to Prince Edward which although better was not really good enough. I discovered late in the year that he had hardly any text books as he was required to share, there being too few to go around. As a result, his performance in 1988 was really poor. This year he will be going to "Christian Brothers College" a private school with fees of Z$550.00 per term plus a few extras. It is supposed to be the best boys' school in Bulawayo so we trust that he will do well. Mark did his grade one music exam and passed and is really enjoying his music. He will miss a term but will start up again once finance permits!

Matthew had a good year in grade 6a and worked

hard. It was also good to see him get into a tennis team soon after learning how to play. He played many matches and enjoyed it. He now has a metal tennis racquet, thanks to Dad! He also played basketball, came 5th place in the cross country and 3rd in high jump. Not too sure who he takes after! He enjoyed learning the recorder taught to him by Mrs. Bruce at Highlands. It is sad that he was unable to finish his last year at Highlands.

Jonathan had a good year in 4a at Highlands and will now go to Hillside with Matthew. One of the things that made 1988 a very good year for him was a boy named Anthony who was his best friend. How they will survive without each other is difficult to imagine. Jonathan played "7-man rugby" in the second term which he really enjoyed. He is really growing and at 9+ is no longer a little boy. (Matthew is now 11+)

For me 1988 was difficult with Mally sick and Mark unhappy at school and many added difficulties. Having sold the car to go to England as a family for a much needed "sabbatical," not only for us but for the children as well; as they are in the firing line as well and bear the burdens unobtrusively too. God very graciously provided us with a car, given to us by Rob Mackenzie. Before we got the car there was a gap where I borrowed cars, hired taxis, walked etc. The V.W. has been a blessing but we had a few problems and with spares difficult to get I have had the car off the road for days at a time. Car problems have characterised 1988, but not only for me but for many in this country ---. It really has helped us personally to have a certain brother in the Lord who has helped us fix the car with no charge and the costs were high. Praise God for such people who obviously do really care ---- and show it.

Bulawayo Assembly is a new Assembly only just 2 years old. It is growing well with around 100 in the meetings *on a Sunday morning. We are trusting the Lord to move into bigger premises possibly next month as the place where we are meeting is inadequate. We are working with Billy and Glenda Nel who are a blessing to the work.*

Although I am the senior minister in Bulawayo and am going to be vitally involved in the Assembly, I will continue to oversee all our churches in Zimbabwe and will be travelling away each month, God willing, for 5 or 6 days taking up to 7 services per trip. A reliable more up to date car is really a great need in order to keep up with such a schedule on a regular basis.

Mally and I will be going to the UK for the month of March, where we are hoping to raise some support towards improving our vehicle situation in Zimbabwe. I was going on my own but have decided to take my wife. I praise God for her, as she has really stood by me during the last few years and I pray God's blessing on her.

One last thing ------.

May 1989 be a year of blessing and outreach for us all and may God prosper us in body, soul and spirit. Thank you for your care.

With love in Jesus.

AB, Mally, and the boys.

Sometime in 1988, before moving to Bulawayo, when visiting the Assembly, I borrowed Billy's lovely old Mercedes and travelled down to my old school at Plumtree. I would have loved to have been able to send Mark to my old school as I had really enjoyed my boarding school years. But despite being very impressed by what I saw, we decided not to send him there. With all that had been going on, and in particular his difficult first year at senior school in Harare, we felt that it would be better for Mark to be at home.

Having decided not to send him to Plumtree, we were encouraged when he was offered a place at 'Christian Brother's College,' which we agreed to accept. It was considered to be the best boys' senior school in Bulawayo at the time. But it was only with reluctance that I allowed my eldest son to attend this Catholic school as I believed that Catholicism was very far from what I understood to be Biblical Christianity.

Both of Billy and Glenda's sons were also students at CBC which gave us some assurance as they would keep an eye out for Mark. But, because he was not starting as a 'first year' student, the only place they could find for him was in a class where most of the boys had no desire to learn. Despite it being a 'good school', it seemed that his second year at high school was also going to be difficult.

Matthew and Jonathan on the other hand were blessed to be able to attend Hillside Junior school which was very close to where we were living. It was at Hillside that Matthew began to excel as a tennis player. Because he had the top Matabeleland Tennis player, in his age group, as a classmate he was greatly assisted in his game. They ended up being on the tennis courts pretty well every day. His classmate received professional coaching every week, and passed on most of what he learned to Matthew who received no coaching except what he received at school. In June 1989, Matthew was awarded his Matabeleland colours from the Junior Tennis Board and played in the Dunlop

Trophy tournament against Mashonaland that month. We were very proud of our young son's achievement.

Our youngest son, Jonathan, got on well at school for which we were grateful. He really loved Rocky his dog and they played hide and seek together, but Rocky always won. The dog was even taken up into a makeshift tree house that the boys built in the front garden.

THE FAMILY 1989

When we moved from Harare, Mally was referred to a specialist in Bulawayo who confirmed the Harare doctor's diagnosis and placed her on certain medication. He said that he believed that she was in the early stages of 'systemic lupus erythematosus.' Naturally we had all been praying about the situation, and I really believed that the Lord had answered our prayers before we left Harare, as after extensive tests when we arrived in England, they said that it was in 'remission.'

ANOTHER TRIP TO ENGLAND.

The main reason for making this trip was to try and raise some outside support for the work in Zimbabwe. It seemed that almost daily we were saying goodbye to long term members of our fellowship which was affecting every congregation around the country. When these people left the country, naturally they took their tithes and offerings with them. But, back in Zimbabwe, our expenses remained the same and so if we were going to survive, we needed to grow rapidly or else receive outside help.

It was true that people were being added to all of our congregations for which we praised God, but not quite as fast as we would have hoped. In addition, it would take time before their 'giving' matched the 'giving' levels of those who had left the country.

During the last 12 months, we had found it difficult to keep a car on the road. I was also aware that most of our ministers had similar problems. But, although getting a 'new' or almost new car in Zimbabwe was difficult, I had been advised that with the right amount of foreign currency we could purchase excellent second-hand cars from Japan! I had even written away to Japan and received a catalogue of reconditioned vehicles with the price of delivery in Zimbabwe, for each one. Sadly, we had no outside resources!

Because he knew about our difficulty in getting

motor vehicles, I had even had a letter from England from Ray Belfield on the subject. He told me about certain vehicles that were available for a very reasonable price. They were surplus army vehicles which would possibly be useful in the rural areas of the country. Sadly, as with the vehicles from Japan, once again it was no use unless we had some foreign currency!

In a bid to raise some foreign currency, I had even written a letter to every contact that I had outside the country. In my letter I explained our situation and asked whether they would personally consider assisting the work in Zimbabwe. In addition, I hoped that they would encourage the church that they attended to adopt us as a missionary endeavour. When I signed my name at the end of the letter, I was sure that I would receive a favourable response. It was not just anyone asking for help, **it was me** someone that they knew, **A.B.Robertson!**

Sad to say, although I did receive a few replies, and a token gift of around Z$5.00 my appeal fell on deaf ears. As a result of the failure of my appeal, I decided to make another trip to the UK as surely there must be churches in the country who would be willing to adopt us as a 'mission' and begin to set aside some funds, to assist the work of God in Zimbabwe that we were part of.

As we would both be away in England, Billy's two older sons moved into our home to care for our boys. They did a good job for which we were very grateful but sadly, whilst we were away, one of our dogs, was either 'dognapped' or managed to get out of the gate and was never seen again. It was Rocky, Jonathan's favourite, a dog that was not yet fully grown. It was a real blow in particular for our sons.

Once again Ray Belfield, or should I say his secretary, arranged ministry for us. As a result, whilst in England we were privileged to visit a total of 15 different fellowships. Sadly, Mally was not able to be with me on each occasion, as at times she was not feeling at all well. Accommodation can be a bit of a problem on these occasions but we had graciously been loaned a house by the Administrator of Wigan Pentecostal Church. His parents had recently been promoted to glory, and the house was empty, so he very kindly let us use it for a week or two which was a great blessing.

We had a very busy month in England, but I will only mention three of the churches we visited. The first was 'Olivet Pentecostal Church' in Ramsbottom in Lancashire, where I spoke at the 'Evergreen Meeting,' held in the afternoon. Sadly, Mally was not with me on this occasion and although I had a bit of trouble finding the church, I managed to arrive just in time. I had a great time ministering to the older members of the fellowship who proved to be very receptive. After the meeting was over, the minister, Paul Andrews, invited me back to their home, where I enjoyed a meal with him and his wife Liz. We got on very well but almost as soon as I finished eating, I had to be on my way to the next meeting which was in Accrington a few miles away.

The second meeting that I would like to mention took place at the Assembly in Preston. This church had an amazing history and was associated with many of the great Pentecostal preachers of the 20th Century. However, when I ministered there in 1989, they had no minister, and the Elders led the meeting. At the close of the meeting, I made an appeal, and it appeared that most if not all of the leaders in the Assembly came up for prayer. I am not sure what touched their hearts that evening but it was a very humbling experience to pray for these well-established, experienced, men of God.

The third and last church that I want to mention was somewhere in the Midlands. I had preached at a church a few miles away, the night before, where the Minister and his wife, had provided us with accommodation. Before we left the next morning this lovely couple made it very clear that we were welcome to return and stay with them for another night. We thanked them for their hospitality, but I assured them that we would be well looked after at the next Assembly as they knew that we required overnight accommodation.

There was a good turnout that evening for a midweek meeting, and we were very well received. Sadly, at the end of the meeting we discovered that our hosts were **not** expecting to provide us with overnight accommodation! Not only that but they seemed decidedly uninterested in where we would spend the night! The minister even suggested that we return to where we had stayed the night before! But it was 9.00pm, and it was a dark, cold, wet, night, and we were completely unfamiliar with the area. Even if we had wanted to, I very much doubt if we would have been able to find our way back to where we had been the night before. It appeared that we would have to find a hotel, or 'bed and breakfast,' but how, on a cold, wet night, in an unfamiliar place?

But our God did not let us down, He is so good! A woman who had attended the meeting that evening, who was a 'lay preacher' with the Methodist Church, happened to overhear the conversation and said, **"You would be very welcome at my home this evening if you would like to come!"**

We naturally did not refuse such a kind offer, and very soon we were on our way to her home. She shared her home with her invalid husband, but it was no trouble for her to open her home to us, even after 9.00pm on a cold, wet evening! In fact, I think that we may well have stayed an extra night in their comfortable and hospitable home, before moving on to our next appointment.

That evening we had a conversation that I will never forget. She was a teacher in a local school, where a young Asian Moslem girl had become pregnant as a result of being raped. When the girl's family discovered that she was pregnant, outside of marriage, they did not try to console her about what had happened, but rather accused her of bringing disgrace on her family. Because the family had been 'dishonoured' it was decided that she would have to die, and an 'accident' was arranged where she was killed by a member of her family.

Our hostess was also a 'counsellor' at the school and the girl had spoken in confidence to her. Although she could not 'prove' that she had been 'murdered,' she was convinced that this is what had taken place because of what the girl had told her! Coming from Zimbabwe, I was horrified that such things could be happening in Britain. I knew that so called 'honour' killings shamefully took place in certain Moslem countries in other parts of the world, but, in the United Kingdom ------that was appalling!!

My friend, Ray Belfield, knew that I was looking for assistance for our work in Zimbabwe and so he set me up with two very good appointments. The first one was with the minister of a very successful Assembly in Nottingham. When I met with -------- I discovered that he was the leader of a growing church that was having a great impact further afield. As with most, if not all AOG Churches in the UK, they were very involved with Missions. Their missionary involvement was assisting congregations in a number of countries overseas.

The question was, what could he do for us? I soon discovered that if he was going to assist us in Zimbabwe, we would need to follow his recommendations, otherwise he was not willing to commit his time and resources to help us. Although I completely understood his point of view, I was not prepared to return to the situation that we had experienced with South Africa previously, and so sadly there was nothing that he could do to assist us.

The other person with whom Ray put me in touch, was a man who had the British Franchise for a Far Eastern Motor Manufacturer. As a result of this franchise, he had become a multi-millionaire in a very short space of time. It appears that one night he awoke in a sweat, as the Lord had challenged him about what he had done with the riches that he had been given? As a result, he had established a 'charity' to assist Christian projects at home and abroad.

As a result of Ray's efforts, I was very privileged to get an interview with his secretary, a man that he had employed to run the charity. I explained our situation in Zimbabwe and he listened very intently and agreed to help us. As a start, they would be willing to provide us with the motor cars that they handled in the UK, at cost price ---- which would be a great saving. In addition, he said that if we were involved in a particular project in Zimbabwe, and I sent him the details, they would consider sponsoring the work.

There can be no doubt that he had made me a very generous offer. I should not have expected anything more, and this offer would have been a real blessing to our work in Zimbabwe if we had been in possession of some foreign currency! As a result, I thanked him for his time and took my leave. As I left, I was beginning to realise that 'raising money' for the work in Zimbabwe was really not my forte. I should have sent someone else as I had not succeeded at all.

But all was not lost as the main reason that we had come to England, at this particular time, was to attend the 'International Gospel Outreach Conference.' which was being held at 'The Hayes Conference Centre' in Swanwick, Derbyshire. My friend, Ray, felt that there was a good chance that one or more of the churches represented at this conference would be happy to support our work in Zimbabwe. Before attending, I had been given to understand that I would be invited to minister at least once, which would give me the opportunity to share the needs of the work in my homeland.

We thoroughly enjoyed the conference, and

were well received by all the delegates. Without going into any details, the conference was very different from any conference that I had ever attended. After a number of meetings had taken place, one of the organisers apologised to me for not giving me an opportunity to address the delegates. He explained that things had developed in an unexpected way but hopefully they would give me an opportunity the following day.

However, that never materialised, and so finally I was told that I would have around 15 minutes to speak at the very last meeting of the conference. I was very disappointed and wondered what I could share in 15 minutes about the work in Zimbabwe that would be meaningful.

Before I tell you what happened in that last meeting, I must first tell you about a struggle that I was having in my own life. Whilst at the conference I realised that if the Lord told me that it was time to leave Zimbabwe, I was not sure that I was willing to obey, as I really loved my country and its people! Yet, if the Lord told me that He wanted me to stay in Zimbabwe, I was not sure that I would be willing to do what He said! As a result of this ongoing battle in my spirit, I found it difficult to sing certain songs during the time of worship. For example, I found it almost impossible to sing,

"I surrender all, I surrender all. All to Jesus blessed Saviour, I surrender all!"

I love singing and I usually sing with all my heart, but I found that I was unable to sing that song. Neither could

I sing,

"Have Thine own way, Lord, have Thine own way;
Thou art the potter, I am the clay;
mould me and make me after Thy will, while I am
waiting, yielded and still."

I was struggling, it was really strange! I was not sure
that I was willing to bend the knee, and do what God
wanted me to do! As a result, I refrained from singing
these songs and others like them.

Once again, in this very last meeting of the
conference, things developed unexpectedly. Around
about the time I may have been invited to address the
conference, a minister who appeared to be well known
to the gathered assembly, got to his feet and went to the
front of the meeting hall. Once there, he began to
'prophesy' over the lives and ministries of certain
people whom he called up to the front.

One of the ministers that he called to the front was
Gary Stevenson who had recently visited Zimbabwe!
When he prayed and prophesied over Gary, I could
identify with what he said, as I knew Gary! He then
called another minister up to the front who was also
known to me, as he had been a missionary in
Zimbabwe! When he prayed and prophesied over this
man, I also believed that it was a word from God,
because of what I knew about him. It was amazing that
he called two men up to the front, out of a couple of
hundred people or more, who were well known to
myself! As a result, by this time, I realised that God was
really using this man.

It was then that he pointed to Mally and myself, and asked us to come up to the front. We were quite surprised as it is something that has only happened to me once or possibly twice during my entire Christian life. Having brought us up to the front he then said something like the following, **"The Lord has shown me that you have climbed many mountains and you will continue to do so. When you arrive at the top of a mountain you will discover that it is not the top, as there will be a valley beyond and then another higher mountain to climb. Once you arrive at the top of the next mountain you will discover that there is yet another even higher peak to climb. However, in time you will be known as an 'overcomer' because you will climb to the top of every mountain that you are required to face."**

Something really happened to me that day as the Holy Spirit spoke through this man. It was amazing! I knew that God had spoken clearly into my situation. Tears filled my eyes and I no longer felt like 'rebelling' against my God. Whatever He wanted me to do I was now willing to do. Praise His wonderful name!

As the meeting was now almost over, the leader of the meeting again apologised to me, and asked if I would close the meeting in prayer. As I faced the congregation with tears in my eyes and with my voice choked up, I said, **"I really do not want to climb any more mountains as I have already climbed quite a few."**

But having said that, I closed the meeting in prayer and the Conference was officially over!

A few days later, we were required to return the car that we had borrowed and then take a coach to the airport. But before doing that we needed to find somewhere to stay overnight, and so we kept a look out for a Bed & Breakfast. It is amazing how many there are, when you are not looking for them, but when you need one, you can't find one. But, eventually, just as it grew dark, we saw a sign and turned off the main road looking for another sign to the B&B. I am not sure how we managed to miss it but it was not long before the road became a country lane and finally it deteriorated into a track. Although we had suspected that we had missed the turning, when the road became a country lane, we were certain that we had missed the turn-off, when it became a farm track!

Sadly, whilst trying to turn around I managed to stall the car and could not get it started again. As a result, we had to walk back up the lane in the dark until we found our destination. Our kindly host then drove me down to the car in his spanking new Jaguar so that I could retrieve our luggage. We had a good night in a lovely home and a great English breakfast in the morning before we set out to sort out the car. As the battery appeared to be flat our host gave us a 'push' in his lovely car, until our car burst into life and we were able to get on our way. I thought that I had made up my mind never to get a 'push' by a car ever again!! Nevertheless, we were very grateful I can assure you!

Once the car was safely returned, we caught a coach to the airport and arrived in plenty of time for our overnight flight back to Harare. But we were in for a shock! When we presented our passports, tickets, and luggage we were told by the kindly British Airways check in clerk that we were not early; in fact, we were 24 hours late! We ought to have caught the flight back to Zimbabwe the evening before! I had it clearly written in my diary that we ARRIVED BACK HOME on the day that we ARRIVED AT GATWICK AIRPORT! What a mistake! Although she was not supposed to do so, she booked us onto a flight back home the following evening for which we were extremely grateful. Once again, the Lord had helped us!

But there were a few problems! For a start, our sons had expected us to arrive home in Bulawayo that evening, but we were still in England! Secondly, Malcolm Fraser would have gone to the airport that morning in Harare to meet us, and on top of that, there was the problem of where to stay for the next 24 hours before our flight home.

Praise God, after a few phone calls, all was sorted. Sadly, by the time we phoned Bulawayo, our sons had already gone to bed wondering what had happened to their parents? My friend Malcolm was very gracious and agreed to come once again to meet the BA flight two days later. Finally, my aunt was willing to receive her nephew and his wife for an unexpected visit and advised us how to get to her home from the airport.

As advised, we were able to catch a bus from the airport which took us to Twickenham where my aunt Diana lived. She graciously put us up for the night and we spent the following day visiting Richmond which turned out to be very enjoyable. Following that, we returned to the airport and had a safe and enjoyable flight home. It was wonderful to be reunited with our family and our two dogs and cat. We were really grateful to the Nel's for their care of our sons and home.

THE FINAL DAYS IN ZIMBABWE!

When we had arrived in Bulawayo just before Christmas, I decided to leave everything exactly the way it was, and not try and impose my leadership upon the work, until after we returned from England. But, although I had made it very clear that I would be the senior minister in Bulawayo, within days of our arrival back from the UK one of the deacons said to me, **"AB, who is leading this work, you or Billy?"**

I was puzzled by his question, as when I had arrived a few months before, I had made it clear that I would be leading the work but my reply was, **"I will meet with the Elders and Deacons after the service on Sunday and let you know!"**

There was no doubt that Billy and Glenda were doing a great job. I realised that if I were to 'lead' the work in Bulawayo, I would have to make a commitment to do so for a minimum of 5 years. But the question was, was I willing to remain in Bulawayo for the next five years? As I meditated upon this, I came to the conclusion that I was not willing to do that, and so I could not 'lead' the work in Bulawayo. That Sunday I spoke to the Elders and Deacons and said something like the following, **"I have decided that I will not be 'leading' the work in Bulawayo and I am happy for Billy to continue to lead the Assembly. I will remain in Bulawayo and continue to lead the movement and perhaps spend time training younger ministers if God opens the way."**

Unbeknown to me at the time, our work in Zimbabwe was coming to an end. We would soon be leaving for the UK.

PROMOTED TO GLORY!

An important commitment holding us in Africa, was my elderly mother who was living in Cape Town! Every year for six years we had made a point of spending our annual holiday in the Cape. In fact, during those years, we always had Christmas lunch with my mother, the residents, and staff at the Bay View Residential home in Muizenburg. We were able to do this largely as a result of the generosity of the assemblies in the Cape. They knew of our situation, and as a result we were able to 'house sit' for various members of the different congregations who went elsewhere for their annual holiday.

One year we even spent our holiday in John Bond's flat in Wynberg for which we were very grateful. It was whilst living in John Bond's flat that our youngest son, Jonathan, gave his heart to the Lord Jesus. My wife, Mally, would every now and then challenge Jonathan to accept Jesus as his Lord and Saviour. However, he would usually flatly refuse! But, one night whilst we were living in Wynberg he said that he would do so. Mally called me into the bedroom and together we led our youngest son to Christ. As a result, both Jonathan and I have our spiritual roots in the Assemblies of God in Cape Town.

There is no doubt that I owe much to my South African brethren. As a result, I want to take this opportunity to thank them for all their love and generosity from which I benefited over many years.

Now, getting back to my mother, I was very concerned for her spiritual well-being! It is true that she had prayed the 'sinners' prayer' with me, some years before, but I was still not convinced that she had really met with the Lord. Each time we visited her, it was difficult to have a meaningful conversation as there were always other residents around and usually the TV was blaring. Well, one day I dropped the family off at the beach and I went to see her on my own. I was thrilled to discover that there was no one around and I had my mother to myself when I arrived and the TV was silent. That afternoon we had a great conversation together and before I left, we prayed. That day my heart was at last at peace, I knew that my mother had committed her eternal destiny to the Lord Jesus and accepted Him as her Saviour!

When we said goodbye, a day or so later, she looked so old and frail that we found it hard to leave. However, I had that assurance in my heart that one day we would meet again at Jesus feet. It was the last time that I saw my mother alive, as she went to be with the Lord on the 4th July 1989.

Although Mally wanted to come with me to the funeral I finally went on my own. In hind sight I do wish that she had come, as she had been such a blessing to my mother. There were only four of us at the funeral, my brother Osmond, my stepsister Daphanie, and my cousin Zeta and I was privileged to take the service.

Although there were only 4 of us at my mother's funeral we need to remember, that the number of people at a funeral does not always reveal the type of life that you have lived. My mother had been a very popular person and had a large number of friends. Sadly, she had been in a nursing home for years, far from the place where she had lived much of her life. In addition, my sister and her family were in Canada, my brother Christopher and his family were in England, my brother Osmond and his family lived a thousand miles away in Johannesburg and we were living in Bulawayo around one thousand, three hundred miles away!

I thank God for both of my parents as they were such a blessing to me!

HOW CAN YOU LEAVE? YOU ARE AN AFRICAN!

It was a busy year as usual but we began to make plans to leave. I made contact with Ray Belfield and he replied by asking me what type of church I wanted. Would I like a church in the country, or in the town? Did I want a large church, or a small church and so on? He had many contacts all over the country and he wanted to do the best that he could for me. In addition to making enquiries all around the UK he made an announcement that we were planning to settle in England at a District Council Meeting of the AOG in the North West.

My new friend, Paul Andrews, asked for my phone number. Since my visit to Olivet Pentecostal Church in Ramsbottom, Paul had accepted an invitation to move to 'Bethshan Tabernacle' in Manchester, and was due to move within a few weeks to take up his new position. He felt that I may be the ideal person to take his place and wondered if I would be interested? When the leaders of Olivet asked him if he had any recommendations about who they should approach to replace him he replied, **"I know a man in Africa --------!"**

However, around this time, back in Bulawayo, we had a visit from Lawrence Wilson who had come up from South Africa. When I told him of our plans to leave Zimbabwe and move to England he said, **"You can't leave Zimbabwe, you are an African! How will you fit in, in the UK?"**

Following my conversation with Lawrence, we had a lot of misgivings, and wondered whether we should call everything off! Both Mally and I, and of course each one of our sons, had been born in Zimbabwe and it was going to be a major upheaval to pack up and leave. As a result, for a short while we were of two minds as to whether to stay or go. When I discussed it with John Baker, he said, **"Why don't you come back to McChlery? If you would like to do that, I could easily go back to Kariba. Think about it, I would be happy to go to Kariba if you want to return to McChlery!"**

It was really good of John to make this offer, but when I considered where I could go if I left Bulawayo, I could not raise any enthusiasm to return to any place that I had been in before, including McChlery. It must be stressed that the money supporting us in Bulawayo · was due to run out at the end of the year. The Assembly in Bulawayo could not support two ministers. If we did not move to the UK we would have to move somewhere, but there was nowhere in Zimbabwe that I felt drawn to at that time!

It was while we were in this period of indecision, that Paul Andrews phoned from England and our youngest son, Jonathan, answered the phone. When Paul mentioned England Jonathan said, **"I do not think we are moving to England, I think we are staying in Zimbabwe."**

I am not sure whether Paul talked with me on that occasion or not. But he made it clear that if we moved to the UK, he would like us to consider Ramsbottom before we considered anywhere else! This I promised to do!

THE HOUSE SALE.

There was no possibility of us taking all our 'furniture' to the UK so we made plans for a 'house sale' to take place on a certain day. But, having never had a house sale before we had no idea what to expect. It was then that Bob Wood, someone from the congregation, asked if we would like a helping hand on the day of the sale. We naturally said yes, and I am so pleased that we did, as we would never have managed without Bob, Sheila and their son Harold.

Pretty well everything had to go, as we were only taking our suitcases with us to England. I remember one man coming in and buying all of my son's comic books. It must have been a very sad day for our sons seeing all their possessions being sold. Not completely sad, as they kept the money that they made from the sale of their personal possessions. It was hard for Mally and I to see items that we had received years before as wedding presents being snapped up. Each one had such a history and many of them were in perfect condition having only been used on special occasions.

We were amazed at how many people showed up as there was a great crowd. It was essential that before anyone left the property, they showed a receipt for the things that they were taking. As a result, I asked our gardener to sit at the gate and not allow anyone to pass the gate without showing him a receipt for the things that they were taking. It was only at the end of the day that I discovered that he could not read or write! So much for our security!!!

At the end of the day, despite at least one person trying to leave the property without paying, we achieved our goal. This particular man tried to leave without paying for an electric drill which was worth a few dollars. Without the help of the Woods, we would have been overwhelmed that day. Praise God for good friends!

THE VICTORIA FALLS.

We were soon to be leaving the country in which we all had been born. It was a country that although changed, we all loved dearly. Following the 'house sale' we now had more than the £1,600 that we were allowed to take out of the country. As a result, we were able to spend a few days at the Victoria falls. We rented a Chalet in the Game Reserve and had a wonderful break.

We were keen to show our sons these magnificent falls before we left the country, as one never knows what the future may hold. As I explained previously, we had taken Mark to the falls when he was 10 months old but that did not count, as he slept right through our visit, and the other two had never been to the falls at all.

We had a lovely time during our short break at the Falls. It was amazing walking through the 'rainforest' and getting completely soaked only to dry out within minutes in the boiling hot sun. Another incredible thing that we saw was that one part of the falls was completely dry. It was not 'global warming,' it just happened to be the time of the year that we were there! Within a few months when the river was at its height, all the falls would be flowing once again! I had seen a photo some years before, that seemed to show a 'dry' Victoria Falls, but it is never completely dry, the photo just showed one section of these amazing 'falls' which are over a mile, wide!

We were in a 'game reserve' and so it was no surprise to see 'warthogs' and other wild animals almost outside our chalet door. We also saw the statue erected to David Livingstone, the great missionary explorer and opponent of the slave trade. While we were there, we visited a 'traditional African Village' that had been constructed to show tourists what village life was like. It proved very interesting and I took pictures of all the family standing outside the different huts. When we moved to England, I told a number of people that they were pictures of our home in Zimbabwe, but later apologised and told them the truth!

We also went to a 'crocodile farm' where we saw crocodiles of all different ages including an enormous beast who went by the name of 'Big Daddy.' While we were there, we were offered the chance to hold a baby crocodile in our hands, but Mally and I were not at all keen. I think all of our sons took advantage of the chance, although I only have a photo of one of our sons holding a baby crocodile.

Over the years, the farm bred many thousands of crocodiles and they were required to return around 10% back into the wild. By the time we visited, instead of crocodiles being an endangered species, they had once again become a bit of a pest in the wild. A very dangerous pest, and one thing is sure, I would not like to meet 'Big Daddy' in the wild!

The boys all acquired tee-shirts while we were there. Some of the shirts had a picture of 'Victoria Falls,' on the front and others had 'Zimbabwe—We Care,' with a Rhino emblazoned on the front. However, whatever else you may be able to do at the famous Victoria Falls, the one thing that is entirely unforgettable is seeing the amazing falls themselves. This spectacular water fall is so much grander than

Niagara, although Niagara is without doubt worth a visit. But Victoria Falls is majestic, in fact it is overwhelming to be exact and we praised God for His goodness in allowing us to see a little more of His wonderful creation in our homeland.

Sadly, our short break was soon over and we had to say goodbye to the Victoria Falls and head back to Bulawayo. We then had to say goodbye to many lovely folks in the Assembly, some whom we had known since 1980 and who had become dear friends. Although Craig and Georgie Friend were not part of the new Assembly, Craig made a point of calling around to see how we were placed financially, for our move to the UK. As it happened, we did not need to call upon his generosity but we were very grateful for his concern.

Among those that we were leaving behind, were Bernard and Ann Maddock, John and Rose Blackmore, Michael and Gladys Morin, Peter, Jenny and Grant Mullin, Bob, Sheila and Harold Wood, Poekie Melville, Ray and Pat Ahton, Eunice and Ndabanengi Busman, and Bert and Kathleen Pring and many others. Last but not least were Geoffrey and Eleanor Mkwanazi a lovely couple who did a great work in Bulawayo and further afield. We valued each and every one and thanked God for having been able to spend a little time with them, before we meet again at Jesus feet.

As we left Bulawayo, it was comforting to know that the Assembly would be well looked after under the ministry of Billy and Glenda Nel and their family. It is amazing to record, that Billy managed to cultivate a good relationship with the minister at Bethshan and our new Assembly eventually moved back into the building. I am not sure when it happened but somewhere along the line, the name of the Assembly changed to 'Revival Ministries.' I had the privilege of preaching at my old church the last time that I was in Bulawayo, which was about 1998. I was thrilled to be able to minister to a large, vibrant, multiracial congregation. Praise God for His faithfulness and praise God that the fellowship is still going strong!

THE FINAL CONFERENCE AT RESTHAVEN.

Before leaving the country, I had arranged a conference at Resthaven just outside Harare. As I look back on the gathering, I am humbled when I realise the people who took the trouble to attend this gathering. I am not able to name them all, but among those who attended were people like Simon Mkolo from Hwange. When I consider the distance that he had to travel, to be present at Resthaven, I am really humbled as Simon was a very busy man of God.

Also present were Peter, Jenny and Grant Mullin, Ted and Freda Anders, and Stan and Marina Anders, Simon and Rina Rhodes, Steve and Linda Bowen, Stuart and Rose MacDonald, Earnest Mutasa, Kesari Dube, Billy and Glenda Nel, John and Sheila Baker, Rob Mackenzie, Rob and Fiona Burns and many more.

In addition to praise and worship and anointed ministry, Rob Mackenzie organised an 'obstacle course' modelled upon a course that he had to do whilst in the army. As can be imagined it turned out to be a real challenge. The whole occasion was a time of great blessing for which we praised God. But all good things finally come to an end upon this planet, and it was soon time to say goodbye which on this occasion was a particularly hard thing to do. It was truly a hard thing to say goodbye as we were leaving Zimbabwe, the land of our birth, most likely, for good!

SOME OF THE MEN I LEFT BEHIND.

However, instead of flying straight to England we had arranged to spend a few days with Mally's brother in Malawi.

OUR MALAWI HOLIDAY.

This was my first visit to Malawi. I had been to South Africa, Botswana, Zambia, Mozambique, and Namibia but I had never been to Malawi so this was a real treat. My brother-in-law was in the tobacco industry and worked for 'Limbe Leaf' a major employer in Malawi. We arrived a couple of days before my birthday (9th of December 1989). They had been living in Malawi for a number of years. They were very good to us and suggested that we spend a couple of days at the Lake, in the 'beach house' that they shared with some other people. As a result, we were driven down to the Lake to enjoy our last couple of days in Africa! The house was literally only a few steps from the beach, and among other things the servant who looked after the house, made us morning or afternoon tea, which he brought down to us on the beach.

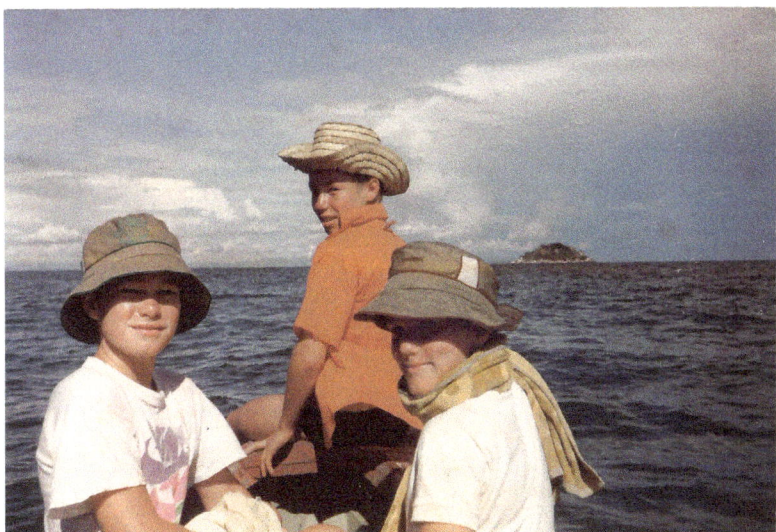

MARK, MATTHEW AND JONATHAN ON LAKE MALAWI

We were joined at the weekend by Rod and Francis and their children, before we had to leave. We could not have had a more wonderful holiday before we left for England but it was soon over and after thanking them for their hospitality we were on our way once again.

ENGLAND.

We enjoyed a pleasant, uneventful, overnight, flight until we were approaching Manchester. We were then informed that our flight had been diverted to Leeds due to a baggage strike in Manchester. Having heard about 'strikes' in the UK for many years, I groaned within myself wondering what we had let ourselves in for! But, in due course we landed safely and then had to go through customs and immigration. Unbeknown to us our son, Matthew, had a sheath knife on his belt which was confiscated by the customs. This did not make our arrival pleasant, for any of us!

Having successfully been through customs and immigration (except for the loss of a valuable knife), we were put on a coach to take us to Manchester airport. It was there that someone from Ray Belfield's congregation in Wigan had agreed to meet us. It was early in the morning on the 11th December 1989, I had just turned 45 years old! It was cold, dark, and raining. As I sat there looking out of the window of the coach at the cold, wet, and dark landscape that was before me, I could not help but compare it with what I had experienced only a few days before. We had spent time swimming in the warm waters of Lake Malawi. In addition, a few days before that, we had enjoyed the conference at Resthaven in the warm summer sun. Less than two weeks before we arrived in England, we had been walking in the rain forest, getting soaked at

Victoria Falls but we had dried out within minutes in the hot summer sun! As I looked out at that dismal early morning scene and meditated on these things, I could not help but say to myself, **"What on earth have I done?"**

EPILOGUE!

After arriving at Leeds airport on that cold, dark, and wet December morning the only Church that I preached at was Olivet Pentecostal Church. This resulted in me becoming their Minister, a position I then held from January 1990 for nine and a half years. It was a good church and a lot happened during that time for which I praise God! I was also very active in the North West Region of the AOG and served on various committees and was even elected as Regional Chairman for a short while. However, I resigned my position as the Minister at Olivet and also as Chairman of the North West Region when we determined to return to Africa, to work with Allan Rockhill for a year in Durban.

But, due to sickness in the family, we never went back to Africa, and after some time doing itinerant preaching, I became the Minister of Bethel Evangelical Church in Preston in September 2001. After just on seven years, I resigned and once again spent a season, where God opened the door for me to preach in Baptist, Congregational, Methodist, Independent, and Pentecostal Churches. Then from September 2013 until the present I have been ministering in Benidorm in Spain. I am the Minister of The English Church, a non-denominational fellowship catering for a small local congregation and the large number of holiday makers who come every year!

Although Mally resumed her nursing career in England (to bring in a little extra money), her health continued to be a problem. She continued working until the year 2001 when she was admitted to the Royal Liverpool Hospital with kidney failure. God was gracious, and in answer to prayer, and the wonderful care of all the staff at the hospital, she miraculously survived. It was quite a miracle when she was finally able to live without dialysis, Despite being on dialysis for six months!

Sadly, only five months after we moved to Benidorm in September 2013, she contracted pneumonia which proved too much for her body, leading to her needing dialysis once again. My wife of just over 39 years went home to glory on 12th January 2014, and was sorely missed.

This was not the only loss that I experienced after leaving Zimbabwe, as sadly our middle son Matthew died tragically on the 17th September 2003. He had been such a blessing to all of us and we were broken-hearted when he died!

Moving on from there, I praise God that our eldest son, Mark, is gainfully employed, and that he and his wife Rebekah have two sons. Our youngest son, Jonathan, is also blessed with a good job and he and his wife Rachel have two sons and a daughter. Praise God, that in these dangerous days, we can pray to God for our families, knowing that they love the Lord!

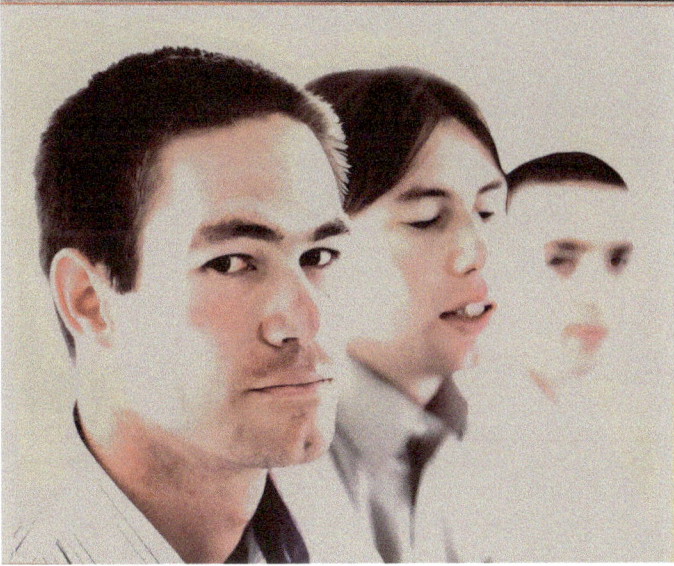

MARK SEPTEMBER 2003.

MATTHEW SEPTEMBER 2003.

JONATHAN SEPTEMBER 2003.

ALAN (AB) and MALLY NOVEMBER 2005

Finally, I want to thank God for blessing me with another 'help meet' even though I am no longer a young man! My wife, Christine, and I were married in the Church of Scotland in Gibraltar on 1st July 2017. We are hoping to relocate to Yorkshire in England early in 2021 but it is all in God's hands. In case you are wondering, I am not retiring, just relocating and ready for whatever God still has, for me to do!

In the service of the King,
Alan (AB) Robertson
Website: - http://bit.ly/ABROBERTSON
 email: - abrobertson9@outlook.com